# MIMESIS
## INTERNATIONAL

**ATMOSPHERIC SPACES**
n. 14

### What is an "Atmosphere"?

According to an aesthetic, phenomenological and ontological view, such a notion can be understood as a sensorial and affective quality widespread in space. It is the particular tone that determines the way one experiences her surroundings.

Air, ambiance, aura, climate, environment, genius loci, milieu, mood, numinous, lived space, Stimmung, but also Umwelt, ki, aida, Zwischen, in-between – all these words are names hiding, in fact, the founding idea of atmospheres: a vague ens or power, without visible and discrete boundaries, which we find around us and, resonating in our lived body, even involves us.

Studying atmospheres means, thus, a parte subjecti, to analyse (above all) the range of unintentional or involuntary experiences and, in particular, those experiences which emotionally "tonalise" our everyday life. A parte objecti, it means however to learn how atmospheres are intentionally (e.g. artistically, politically, socially, etc.) produced and how we can critically evaluate them, thus avoiding being easily manipulated by such feelings.

Atmospheric Spaces is a new book series whose aim is to become a point of reference for a community that works together on this philosophical and transdisciplinary subject and for all those whose research, more broadly, is involved in the so-called "affective turn" of the Social Sciences and Humanities.

OLA SIGURDSON

# ATMOSPHERES IN EVERYDAY LIFE

## On Existential Spatiality

This volume is published with the support of the Department of Literature, History of Ideas, and Religion at the University of Gothenburg, Sweden.

# CONTENTS

$$1.$$

LITERARY EVOCATIONS OF ATMOSPHERE

The word atmosphere comes from the Greek *atmos*, vapour, and *spharia*, sphere, and literally means a sphere of vapour. Our globe is surrounded by just such a sphere of vapour, which, in addition to water vapour, consists mainly of nitrogen and oxygen. Without the atmosphere, we could not live. It protects us from ultraviolet radiation and reduces the temperature difference between night and day. But the word is also used to describe another phenomenon that can be said to surround us in a similar way, though the focus is experiential rather than scientific. For example, there is a special atmosphere that prevails on a late spring evening walking home through Gothenburg, Paris or Rome. It is atmosphere in this sense that this book concerns itself with. Certainly, there are those who can live without the special atmosphere of a late spring evening in Gothenburg, but could we live without atmospheres at all? Wouldn't we miss out on all that gives a world face and flesh, all that makes this place where we live a world?[1] Though the importance of atmospheres is easier to capture, it is more difficult to establish what they are made of and where we find them.

Atmosphere in this second sense has in recent decades become a frequently used and even debated concept in philosophy, literary studies, architectural theory, design, urban planning and theology. The concept of atmosphere developed here refers to an essential experience of the atmosphere of space that can nevertheless be difficult to put into words. Like the earth's atmosphere, the atmospheres studied by philosophers and architects but also designed by interior designers and scenographers are characterised by the fact that their boundaries are not fixed and clear but become increasingly thin the further out into the periphery of the atmosphere we go. In other words, it is not a fixed thing that we can see from a distance, but neither is it a purely subjective feeling. The atmosphere during my late evening walk through Gothenburg, Paris or Rome is something that

---

1    Thibaud 2015, p. 7.

affects me, not something I evoke within myself. Unlike the layer of gas that surrounds the earth, the city's atmosphere is certainly something that must be studied from within as an experience, but at the same time, like the earth's atmosphere, something that surrounds us. The French equivalent of the atmospheric term, *ambiance*, derives from the Latin *ambire*, which means to enclose. One of the defining characteristics of atmospheres is that they envelop us.

If atmospheres envelop us, how does an author introduce themself to atmospheres? Shouldn't atmospheres be something we discover, become aware of or even suffer from? Surely an introduction presupposes that we get to know something that was previously unknown to us? Instead, I want to start with the important distinction between the phenomenon and the concept: it is one thing to experience an atmosphere and another to reason about this atmosphere using phenomenology and architecture. But if the experience of atmospheres as phenomena is to be explored, it becomes crucial not to let our reflections on atmospheres determine in advance which of these phenomena should be articulated and which should be bypassed or ignored. Phenomenology has therefore emphasized that the study of atmospheres should start from how they have come to be articulated in everyday language since this reflects an ambiguous yet rich experience of atmosphere that people actually make and have.[2] The quest to understand the phenomenon of atmosphere should therefore stick to the phenomenon and listen to the concrete experiences of it. In order to introduce the concept of atmosphere, it is important to also try to understand the atmospheres that surround us. One of the points of thinking about atmosphere as a concept is that it helps us to articulate the phenomenon and therefore also to both understand and experience it in a more conscious and perhaps more nuanced way.

This is where fiction, as well as images, can help us. Both not only present us with an atmosphere but also evoke it in us in some sense, at least by associating it with atmospheres we ourselves have experienced at some point. Literature, like images, is not only about understanding something but also about being touched or moved by an atmosphere. I will briefly mention and comment on three fictional passages, not to analyse them in depth but, rather, to evoke in the reader some associations with how atmospheres can envelop us as a background to the more theoretical introduction to the concept. Images could serve the same purpose; they evoke atmospheres as well.

---

2    Böhme 2013, p. 50.

The French writer Antoine de Saint-Exupéry (1900–1944), best known for his children's book *The Little Prince*, was also an experienced and adventurous aviator. He described his earlier experiences of flying in Africa and South America in a number of internationally acclaimed novels where the appeal, apart from the purely suspenseful aspects, often lies in their depictions of atmosphere, as in this introduction to *Southern Mail*:

> A sky as pure as water bathed the stars and brought them out. And then night fell. Dune by dune the Sahara unfolded itself beneath the moon. Its light, falling on our foreheads with the pallor of a lamp which blends the softened forms, enveloped every object in its velvet sheen. Under our soundless footsteps the sand had the richness of a carpet. And bare-headed we walked, freed of the cruel weight of the sun. In that dwelling place – the night ...[3]

Here, Saint-Exupéry depicts a peaceful atmosphere created by the starry sky and the moonlit dunes that transforms matter itself into something delicate. But tranquillity is threatened in the very next sentence – "Yet how could we trust this peacefulness?" – because the trade winds "flowed restlessly towards the south". For the aviator, wind, especially strong wind, is a source of anxiety. The author here presents the peaceful mood by describing how the desert landscape and natural light relate to each other. The human figures that appear in this introduction are described as those who can relate to the atmosphere but not a part of its origin. At the same time, it is through these figures that we experience some of the particular sensual qualities that are also part of the atmosphere: the steps become softer, and the headgear is removed because protection from sun and wind is not needed. At least two, probably three senses are mentioned: hearing, sight and, in a sense, touch. The introduction ends with a lyrical exclamation, "In that dwelling place, the night ..." (ellipses in original), where the author's alter ego is almost seized by the mood of the scene. However, at the same time the narrator is clear to the reader, commenting from a distance on the atmosphere that is depicted. An atmosphere is painted in which the author himself – as well as the reader indirectly – is enveloped by the atmosphere.

In his introduction, Saint-Exupéry sets the stage for what is to come. Even for those of us with limited experience of desert landscapes, there is something familiar to relate to, namely the stars and the night, which are conventional symbols of a particular atmosphere.[4] The focus on night and

---

3    Saint-Exupéry 2000, p. 11.
4    Böhme 2001, p. 46.

its atmospheric quality becomes clear through the author's exclamation. At the same time, the text turns the peacefulness of the night into something a little different or even mysterious: the desert becomes, at least for some of us readers, something relatively unknown. But above all, the objects appear literally and figuratively in a different light than in the day: they are no longer things represented by harsh sunlight as solid objects but things whose "softened forms" are "blended" and "enveloped" and appear as less demarcated from each other and from the surroundings than before. The mood that the passage conveys, where the staging is not independent of the figures tramping about in the dunes, is of a peace that also carries something unknown.

In her poem "Cornwall", the American poet and Nobel Prize laureate Louise Glück (1943–2023) describes someone who has suffered from writer's block and, in her quest to find her way back to her writing, first ventures out into the countryside but eventually returns home to the city and moves her chair out onto the balcony. Here we encounter a cityscape rather than a desert landscape, perhaps New York given Glück's own birthplace:

> The streetlights were coming on,
> lining the side of the river.
> The offices were going dark.
> At the river's edge,
> fog encircled the streetlights.
> One could not, after awhile, see the lights
> but a strange radiance suffused the fog,
> its source a mystery.
>
> The night progressed. Fog
> swirled over the lit bulbs.
> I suppose this is where it was visible;
> elsewhere, it was simply the way things were,
> blurred where they had been sharp.[5]

In the passage, twilight turns to night; here, the artificial light from the streetlamps is enveloped in a dense fog that eventually becomes a luminosity without a visible source. As the offices darken, existence becomes less sharp, more blurred. Here, the changing ratios of light come into focus even more than in the passage by Saint-Exupéry, but where in his case the particular light gave things a certain delicate quality, in Glück's case

---

5    Glück 2014, p. 29.

the blurriness of things instead seems to be a source of disillusionment, perhaps even uncanniness.

Glück also uses common experiences and accepted ways of portraying them to convey a certain mood. Both twilight and fog are atmospheric phenomena *par excellence*.[6] Both are natural phenomena, and both have the enveloping character that more generally characterises atmospheres. In this case, the natural phenomenon is made visible by the artificial light of the streetlamps; as the poem notes, it is precisely here that something becomes visible that is always the case. Twilight and fog are not only natural phenomena but also phenomena that affect those who are enveloped by them. Precisely because of the specific light produced by these natural phenomena, the outside world becomes more uncertain for the enclosed subject, who is therefore instead referred back to itself. The uncertainty at issue here is not simply an uncertainty as to whether something is one way or the other; it is an affectively tuned uncertainty that is experienced as a tone that permeates the entire room. This fits well with the reason why a poet uses a mood-setting image in their poem, not just as a metaphor for an inner event but as a depiction of how the person enveloped by twilight and fog is affectively and physically influenced by them, allowing them to come into a mood of uncertainty that affects their whole of existence. Twilight and fog are indeed phenomena that can be seen, as when "fog encircled the streetlights", but at the same time they encompass a broader register than the sense of sight. Likewise, the poem makes this uncertainty visible to the reader in a way that touches much more than just the understanding of the image by evoking affective charge; the description touches the reader.

Twilight and fog can put those who are surrounded by them in a romantic mood. In the passage by Saint-Exupéry above, where, although there is no fog, twilight and night bring a similar uncertainty, it is possible to speak of the peace that has mysterious elements as a romantic atmosphere. With Glück, it is different; her combination of twilight and fog seems more uncanny, mainly because of the alienation that her depiction of uncertainty brings. The uncanny, like the mysterious serenity of Saint-Exupéry, is a play between the familiar and the strange, but in the uncanny the strangeness takes on a tone of threat, of something that touches deeply on the poet's own ambivalence. There is no regained harmony in this poem. Silence is what remains for the poet laureate: "Ahead, as I have said, was silence."[7]

---

6    See Böhme's discussion of twilight and haze in 2013, pp. 54–75 but also Griffero's discussion of twilight in 2013, pp. 121–134.

7    Glück 2014, p. 29.

An atmosphere of uncanniness also appears in an interesting way in the German author Andreas Maier's auto-fictional work *Die Straße*. Now we are no longer moving in a desert landscape, nor in an atmospheric cityscape, but on a street in a residential area. The spatiality at issue here is an actual house. In the following passage, the author's alter ego describes how the other houses in the neighbourhood, despite their resemblance to his own house or perhaps precisely because of it, fill his ten-year-old self with unease:

> Basically, these houses on Mühlweg and in the Barbara block in general all looked the same. It was monotonous fifties or sixties architecture. But precisely because they all followed the same pattern, the occasional distinctive details of the exterior could give each of them an individual substance so that I never saw the whole street but always these individual households, behind which was a more or less completely isolated world of its own.[8]

The details that distinguish the houses are differences in the colours of the facades, the size and position of the windows, the smells of the houses and whose objects were gathered at the bottom of the staircase. Maier's account refers to multiple senses, telling of a life lived in a different way. As he was enveloped in the "atmosphere of the strange dwelling", "a certain bodily antipathy" was aroused, originating in what he saw, smelled and touched.[9] The thought occurs to him that if he himself had grown up in one of these strange houses, he, too, would have been a different person.

The child's experience of strange houses that Maier depicts in his novel is a good illustration of what Sigmund Freud speaks of as the uncanny, *das Unheimliche*, an experience of something that is familiar and strange at the same time, something that is at once domestic, secret and terrible.[10] What is particularly interesting in this context is that Maier's prose captures how this uncanny atmosphere is anchored in the materiality of the houses and the objects found in them: the strange shoes at the foot of the stairs are experienced as traces of people walking in strange paths and living strange lives despite being only a few meters away from his parents' house. Maier also succeeds in depicting how, for the author's young alter ego, it is above all a bodily experience: body and space belong together through the atmosphere that connects them and which is anchored not just in a single sensory impression but several simultaneously, a kind of synesthesia.

---

8    Maier 2015, p. 7. My translation.
9    Maier 2015, p. 9.
10   See Freud 1955.

Each house constitutes "a more or less completely isolated world of its own" and the child experiences purely sensory-bodily rather than reflects cognitively on the fact that he himself would have been someone else if he had grown up in one of these alien houses with their alien atmospheres. Notice the sequence: here it becomes clear that space, although in these cases obviously created by the people who built the houses and who inhabit them, nevertheless in another sense shapes the bodies before they shape the rooms. Although not completely deterministic, space, by virtue of the atmosphere, has power over the body in a way that is impossible to resist in the first place.

The passage from Maier's novel manages to capture something of the effect of the atmosphere on us, and he anchors this effect in the specific and material. At the same time, the narrative also raises the question of how private the experience of a particular atmosphere really is. Reasonably, the alien dwelling should not be alien to the person who actually lives there, which would mean that the uncanny atmosphere in fact falls back on the individual who temporarily encounters it. But if this were so, how could the "atmosphere of the strange dwelling" arouse a "bodily antipathy" in the young Maier? Is it perhaps rather the experience of a home as familiar and a strange house as uncanny that is the common factor? Do we share atmospheres with each other, or do they set us apart? Are they rooted in things, in ourselves as individuals or somewhere in between?

Of course, reading about an uncanny atmosphere is not the same as experiencing such an atmosphere myself any more than I can sense the smell of rain on asphalt just because I read about rain on asphalt. Here, inevitably, a media shift is taking place.[11] But literature also has the power to use the imagination – in the sense of being able to imagine that something is different, but also to empathize with it – to put the reader in a certain mood. Literature here is not about representing an extra-literary reality to a greater or lesser extent (or not at all), but above all about affecting the reader. A clear example is horror literature: its purpose is undoubtedly not only to tell of horrific events but also to terrify. This means that the literary text itself can be said to strive in some sense to carry the characteristics of the mood it wants to evoke in the reader. Stephen King's novels are not only about horror but are themselves uncanny, not just in their content but also in their literary form. In the case of literature, it does not have to overwhelm us in the same way as an atmosphere that dominates the world

---

11　Fischer-Lichte 2008, pp. 75–76.

around us; instead it can move us, affectively as well as physically, if we are swept up in its power.[12]

By depicting atmospheres in words, these literary examples can not only help to put us in a particular mood and give words to it, but words can also be used outside literature as well when we ourselves are affected by a mood in the spaces we inhabit. Writing has provided insights into the nature of atmospheres and at the same time posed several questions in response to them. Atmospheres seem to have to do with spatiality, whether it is about landscapes or houses, and the things that make up space. They engage our senses and our physicality. We are affected by them, as if they were external forces, but in that they are atmospheres for us, they also seem to be dependent on us. Their presence is palpable yet elusive, distinct yet often mundane to the point of unnoticed. Not least, they draw our attention to the question of how to conceive of the relationship between ourselves, the world we inhabit and the language through which we articulate that very relationship. What kind of beings must we humans be in order to experience atmospheres? How is the world constituted so that the experience of atmospheres is possible? And what possibilities do we have to understand these through language? In other words, the attempt to articulate atmospheres as phenomena leads us to the philosophical question of our own relationship to the world while also dealing with aesthetics in a very broad but, at the same time, concrete sense. It means interrogating how we perceive the world and how the world affects us. The question of how we create a comfortable atmosphere in our home or an inviting atmosphere in our city is therefore not independent of how we think about human beings and their relationship to their world – and vice versa. It may be worth mentioning here that atmospheric studies of these relationships should be understood as *critical* investigations. The question of this scholarship is not only how human beings, world and language relate to each other but also how the prevailing understanding of this relationship may conceal our human attempt to gain control over our environment by displacing the atmospheres, reducing them to a part of our inner emotional life.

Introducing atmospheres in a way that does justice to the phenomenon and pursues a more conceptual understanding of it requires a movement between the concrete and the categorical. The concrete literary passages touched upon here raise questions of a categorical nature. The conceptual exercises capture and deepen these questions, so that we can better

---

12    Gumbrecht 2012, p. 18.

understand the concrete atmospheres we encounter in these texts and, above all, in our own lives. I am writing this book because I myself am someone who is surrounded by atmospheres, and I want to try to understand them and also relate to their concrete manifestations in a more critical and constructive way. The fact that atmospheres seem so elusive has more to do with their ubiquity, almost as a tacit condition of our lives, than with their being particularly alien to us in general. In the spirit of phenomenology, I will turn not only to the atmospheres themselves but also to my own experiences, even when dealing with more categorical, philosophical questions. Thus, the essay, in the sense of a test, appears to be the appropriate form for such an attempt. As one of the leading figures of atmospheric philosophy, Gernot Böhme, has pointed out, the time is not yet ripe for systematic accounts of the philosophy of the atmospheres.[13] And perhaps the time will never be ripe, given the ephemeral nature of atmospheres.

My second chapter begins by presenting the prehistory of the phenomenological concept of atmosphere and its most prominent predecessors in philosophy. This also gives me an opportunity to nuance the differences between some terms that I have used here almost synonymously: atmosphere and mood. In the same chapter, a summary of the phenomenological concept of atmosphere follows, drawing attention to the questions already posed by the literary passages. The third chapter addresses the question of how we relate to atmospheres in a way that is both constructive and critical. On the one hand, atmospherology itself is a critical reckoning with what it perceives as a reductive understanding of our world of experience. On the other hand, there is reason to critically examine what atmospheres do to us and the degree to which we can distance ourselves from them – there is no reason to believe that all atmospheres are edifying. Here, of course, the question arises not only of how we experience atmospheres and what they are, as covered in Chapter 3, but also, and above all, how we produce atmospheres. This question is then explored in greater depth in Chapter 4, which focuses on how the concept of atmosphere is used in the field of architecture. Further, in Chapter 5, I tackle the broad topic of how we actually live in atmospheres by moving inside and out, from the home to the city to nature. The sixth chapter concerns "numinous edifices", taking the experience of two sacred buildings in Rome as paradigmatic examples of the overwhelming quality

---

13    Böhme 2019a, p. 11. Cf. the more general discussion of conceptuality in Blumenberg 2018.

of atmospheres. The seventh and final chapter of the book shows why atmospheres concern us in our everyday lives through an ethnographic account of walking in the city.

2.

**ATMOSPHERE AND PHENOMENOLOGY**

Atmospheres are everyday phenomena. But despite, or perhaps because of, their ordinariness, they do not seem to be easy to account for or sometimes even to notice.[1] Whether vagueness is part of the nature of atmospheres or whether it is rather due to the ambiguity of everyday language is an open question. In any case, in philosophy, and more recently in phenomenology in particular, there has been an effort to gain greater clarity in the matter. As will be shown, "atmosphere" has much in common with "mood" (in German, *Stimmung*); the first half of this chapter will therefore explore the partial common history of these two terms in a way that also clarifies the differences between them. The purpose of a more precise concept of atmosphere is to get to the heart of the matter, atmosphere as a phenomenon. A successful atmospheric concept is one that helps us to better articulate the atmospheres that have always touched us, are touching us, or will touch us. The second half of the chapter is therefore a description of the atmosphere as a phenomenon using the established concept. The literary examples of atmospheres in the opening chapter posed questions for us about atmospheres that I hope to answer to some extent here.

*Atmosphere as a Concept*

The story begins with mood or *Stimmung*. The meaning of *Stimmung* may seem as elusive as the meaning of the term "atmosphere". This is partly because in everyday language, at least in our time, "mood" is used almost as a synonym for "atmosphere". The conceptual history of *Stimmung* is close to the scope of the concept of atmosphere, although it is drawn

---

1 On the vagueness of atmospheres, see Griffero 2010, pp. 3–10; Rauh 2012, pp. 177–202.

from a different sphere of experience: music rather than meteorology.[2] In music, since at least the sixteenth century, the term *Stimmung* [tuning] has referred to either an activity, tuning an instrument; a result, that the tuned instrument sounds good; or a relationship, that the parts of the instrument are harmoniously in tune with each other or the whole instrument with the other instruments in an orchestra. When we talk about the "tone" of a room or of ourselves being "in tune" with something today, the associations can still move into the realm of music. The fact that we speak of "mood music" indicates both a superimposition of meanings and a quality that in some sense lies between the subjective and the objective. We use mood music to "get into the mood". Thus, it is both something that concerns myself and something that originates somewhere else than myself. Perhaps "mood", more than "atmosphere", approaches a subjective position: it makes more sense to speak of "my mood" than of "my atmosphere". But as long as the musical associations resonate with the use of *Stimmung*, the term can hardly be understood as entirely subjective. As a first violinist in an orchestra, to speak of "my *Stimmung*" would not inspire much confidence. Even in an emotional sense, mood or *Stimmung* is primarily something we relate to, not something we produce on our own.

At the time of German Romanticism, towards the end of the eighteenth century, when the term was taken from the sphere of music to be used also for the aesthetic experience, its meaning underwent an interesting shift. Gradually, *Stimmung* became detached from its "objective" meaning in music and became more and more an expression of the human interior. Finally, in the twentieth century, the term reached beyond the opposition between subject and object.

Romanticism is thus the first stage in this shift in meaning. Here we see how the concept becomes increasingly internalized, and its relationship to the self moves from a certain distance between something objectively given and the subject to become something more intimate: in Immanuel Kant's famous *Critique of Judgement* from 1790, *Stimmung* is about the relationship between the human being's imagination and understanding and how these two radiate together in the judgement of taste; in a letter from 1795 by Friedrich Schiller, the term stands for a determination of mind and reason as well but also as something that characterizes the human mind as a whole; in G. W. F. Hegel's writings in the 1820s and 30s, it concerns

---

2    For longer historical perspectives on *Stimmung*, see Spitzer 1963, and for an aesthetic conceptual history, see Wellbery 2010, pp. 703–733. For a brief conceptual history of atmosphere, see Riedel 2019, pp. 85–95. Spitzer 1942, pp. 169–218 also conveys interesting views, as does Thibaud 2015a, pp. 13–43.

"the innermost and most proper" of subjectivity, namely the relationship to oneself.[3] The journey towards the inner self of the human being seems to be complete. But when we reach 1878, Friedrich Nietzsche has taken a different turn, and *Stimmung*, in defiance of the increasing internalization, comes to stand for a process outside of the self rather than something that characterizes our interior.[4] Here, through the body and language, the complex of moods opens us to dimensions of life that allow us to say goodbye to the fiction of the self.

Eventually, phenomenologists such as Moritz Geiger, Martin Heidegger and Otto Friedrich Bollnow come to understand *Stimmung*, beyond any talk of inner versus outer or subjective versus objective, as a fundamental determinant of human existence as such. Through anxiety, Heidegger argues in *Being and Time* (1927), our fundamental freedom and, thus, vulnerability as human beings is revealed in a way that precedes any reflection; Bollnow objected in *Das Wesen der Stimmungen* (1941) that even happier moods reveal something about the fundamental existence of human beings.[5] Whether Bollnow's objection to Heidegger actually applies to his phenomenology we can leave unsaid – Heidegger later came to discuss other possibilities of existence as well. However, we can conclude that both Heidegger and Bollnow understood the concept of *Stimmung* as something beyond the opposition between subject and object, namely a phenomenon in which our human being-in-the-world, our existence, can both be experienced as such but also become known to us. By understanding *Stimmung* or mood as a kind of pre-reflexive matrix from which a more reflexive differentiation between feeling and understanding can emerge, they, like several other phenomenologists, describe a culmination of the history of the philosophical or aesthetic concept of *Stimmung*.

The main purpose of my brief sketch of the evolution of this term is to give an idea of how the concept of mood has, since German Romanticism, been a central way of formulating different understandings of the relationship between human beings, the world and language, going beyond a simple binary opposition between what is considered to belong to the subjective and what is considered to belong to the objective. Mood is found at the intersection of ourselves and the world. In this way, as we will soon see, the concept of mood is similar to the concept of atmosphere and can also be understood as one of its predecessors, although it derives from

---

3    Kant 2000, p. 104 [§9]; Schiller 2002, letter 20; Hegel 1990, p. 447.
4    Nietzsche 1996, §§13–14.
5    Heidegger 1977, §40; Bollnow 2009, pp. 29–36, 47–59, 67–71 *et passim*.

music rather than meteorology. But are music and meteorology really two separate fields? In ancient times, music was not only about the experience of auditory tones but also, and above all, about the harmony that was said to exist between the different spheres. Even the history of the concept of mood goes back to these notions of world harmony, where the harmony of the auditory tones would reflect the harmony between the spheres and the correspondence between the macrocosm and the microcosm. So perhaps atmospheres have more to do with moods than we think? At the same time, today mood is no longer used exclusively for a certain harmonious mood, as a situation lacking this mood would therefore lack any mood at all. Mood, like atmosphere, is used, at least in phenomenology, as a general, descriptive concept of the mood that characterises a particular situation, not as a normative concept. Moodlessness is also a mood, so to speak.

The history of the term also shows why mood can be understood as both a competitor and a precursor to atmosphere. First, it relates to an affective dimension of the self but is also an overall determination of ourselves. Second, mood is not only about the self but also about something that surrounds us, like an atmosphere, and allows us to "get in the mood". Third, mood is pre-reflexive, meaning that it is immediately given with our existence and only secondarily subject to our reflection. A human being is in an eminent sense, at least according to the phenomenologists, a mood being. The fictional examples of atmospheres in the first chapter can equally well illustrate these three points about mood. Hereafter, however, mood will be discussed more in relation to the ego pole, the subjective end of the spectrum, and atmosphere more in relation to the object pole, the objective end of the spectrum. Nevertheless, the conceptualisation of the phenomenon in question here has a history that precedes the contemporary use of atmosphere in phenomenology.

As a sample from phenomenology after Heidegger, we can first note that Maurice Merleau-Ponty in his *Phenomenology of Perception* (1945) uses the term *atmosphére* for a sensory experience that is located *between* subject and object and that sets the horizon for both.[6] *Atmosphére is* used quite extensively in *Phenomenology of Perception* to refer to a horizon that surrounds us, without making the concept the subject of any particular conceptual enquiry. Then we can also note that Elisabeth Ströker in *Philosophische Untersuchungen zum Raum* (1977) speaks of the "tuned" or "mood" space (*der gestimmte Raum*) as an aspect of the lived space. In contrast to the "spectator space", the observed space, which is characterised

---

6     Merleau-Ponty 1945, pp. 262–263.

by measurability, the tuned space is a space that is "atmospheric" in quality, that is, immediately given as an existentially conditioned space where we hope or fear, feel at home or alienated, love or hate.[7] In short, the existential spaces we inhabit are tuned to a certain tone or mode that colour our experience of them and gives our existence its fundamental and inescapable emotional quality. Merleau-Ponty and Ströker make clear how both "mood" and "atmosphere" play central roles in post-Heideggerian phenomenology, without being the centre of its interest. On the one hand, their use concerns the same kind of phenomena, but on the other hand, no fixed and elaborate terminology is suggested.

The moment when the concept of atmosphere gains greater firmness and also comes closer to the centre of phenomenological interest is probably Hermann Schmitz's 1969 book, *Der Gefühlsraum,* where mood and atmosphere are determined in relation to each other, but atmosphere becomes the overriding concept.[8] While Schmitz (1928–2021), like phenomenology as a whole from Heidegger onwards, turned to the task of philosophically analysing everyday experience, to my knowledge no other phenomenologist has devoted themself to system-building in the same way as Schmitz. His ten-volume *System der Philosophie* runs at over 5,000 pages and deals not only with space but also with presence, the body, the person and the sublation of presence.[9] More than five volumes are devoted to spatiality, but the centre of Schmitz's philosophy can be said to be the living body, which is intimately and inseparably linked to spatiality in the concept of situation that is crucial to Schmitz's philosophy.

In phenomenology, a general distinction is made between two aspects of corporeality, namely between the lived and experienced body (*der Leib*), and the body as a physical object (*der Körper*). For Schmitz, too, it is the human experience of being a corporeal being that is at the centre of his philosophical interest.[10] The so-called Cartesian dualism, the understanding of human existence as consisting of body and soul, is therefore fundamentally questioned by Schmitz in favour of a bodily existence, the main characteristic of which is the immediate experience of bodily feelings and movements such as pain, hunger, fatigue, joy and grief, but also jumping, dancing, breathing and swallowing. It is from the first-person experience that we primarily understand what it means to be a bodily being, not by viewing the body as an object from a third-person

---

7    Ströker 1977, p. 22.
8    Schmitz 2019b, pp. 259–260.
9    Schmitz 2019f.
10   Schmitz 2019c.

perspective. A central concern of Schmitz's entire philosophical enterprise is to re-establish the importance of the original and immediate experience of being a living, bodily being in a world that claims us, an experience that he argues has been marginalised throughout the history of the West, with a few exceptions. This marginalisation goes back much further than Descartes to Greece in 400 BCE. This historical mistake, which Schmitz summarises as the "psychological-reductionist-introjectionist" reification of the world, has prevailed since Democritus and Plato, but it also continued through medieval Christianity into modern science.[11] His somewhat obscure term simply refers to the fact that all feelings, moods and atmospheres are supposedly relegated to the human mind, rather than being found where our experience tells us they really belong, namely in space and the body. The reification of the world and the consequent internalisation of the emotions helps us to gain mastery over both the external and the internal world. We defend ourselves against the atmospheres by trying to deprive them of their power over us in a supposed act of internalisation.

Schmitz's philosophical system forms the basis for a movement in phenomenology that Schmitz himself has chosen to call "new phenomenology".[12] What is new in the new phenomenology is above all an increased emphasis on overcoming the gap between subject and object. The "old" phenomenology, according to Schmitz, through its focus on intentionality – that human consciousness is directed towards the things in the world and is thus active – failed to recognise the passivity of human life experience and thus, more or less involuntarily, maintained the historical difference between human bodily experience and the world, or between subject and object. However, our fundamental experience of the world includes being passively gripped by external forces, forces that we cannot control. When the ancient Greeks of Homer's time understood themselves as being under the sway of *ares* or *eros* – that is, the god of war Ares or the god of love Aphrodite – or the early Christians saw themselves as being gripped by *pneuma*, the Holy Spirit, they were not mistaken except insofar as they maintained a mythological personification of these powers. Personification (for which not all ancient thinkers are to be blamed, according to Schmitz) would then involve a similar mistake to the introjectionist localisation of the emotions to the interior, namely, attributing them to the interior of someone else.[13] In fact, *ares as* well as

---

11    See, for example, Schmitz 2016.
12    See, for example, Schmitz 2003, but also Griffero 2019, pp. 9–41.
13    See, above all, Schmitz 2019a, pp. 146–153.

*eros* and *pneuma* could be described as atmospheres in Schmitz's sense: powers poured into space that envelop and grip the body.[14]

Schmitz has repeatedly lamented that the phenomenological tradition has not listened to the theologian and scholar of religion Rudolf Otto, who coined the term "the numinous" to refer to the alien and overwhelming aspect of the sacred, thus emphatically breaking with any idea of reducing the sacred to an inner feeling.[15] According to Otto in *The Idea of the Holy* (1917), the numinous is something "outside the self", and although Otto refers to the divine and not to atmosphere, the divine, like atmospheres, cannot be reified because it is something "wholly other".[16] In Schmitz's eyes, this makes him an ally against the introjectionists. And rightly so – I will return to Otto in more detail in Chapter 6.

Other thinkers allied with Schmitz's critique of introjectionism, including Goethe, particularly through his theory of colour, the French psychiatrist Eugène Minkowski through his emphasis on lived experience and also the German graphologist and philosopher Ludwig Klages and his emphasis on human passivity. Neither Edmund Husserl, the founding figure of modern phenomenology, nor Heidegger, nor even Merleau-Ponty can live up to the necessary break with the psychological-reductionist-introjectionist reification, Schmitz argues, because they maintain the distance between subject and object in different ways.[17] As a result, they never achieve phenomenology's goal of turning to the things themselves, which is why he calls his philosophical proposal a *new* phenomenology. In this new phenomenology, the centre of a human being's "spontaneous life experience" (*die unwillkürliche Lebenserfahrung*) is to be "affectively overwhelmed" (*das affektive Betroffensein*) by atmospheres.[18] Schmitz describes his new phenomenology as being as empirical as natural science in its endeavour to be faithful to spontaneous life experience, and therefore it becomes neither speculative nor metaphysical in its intention. However, his concern is not only descriptive but also critical, insofar as it is to re-establish this experience and thus counteract the colonisation of the lifeworld by a reifying and dualistic concept. Despite his rather traditionalist conception of what a philosophical system should be, Schmitz emerges as both an original and, in some sense, a radical thinker. How "new" his phenomenology really is in relation to the "old" phenomenology I will leave

---

14    See Schmitz 2016, p. 30 and Schmitz 2019b, pp. 98–133.
15    Schmitz 2019a, pp. 74–75.
16    Otto 2014, pp. 11, 76.
17    Schmitz 2003, pp. 1–8.
18    Schmitz 2003, p. i, ii.

unsaid and instead speak in the following paragraphs of atmospherology in relation to this version of phenomenology.

The most well-known of the philosophers inspired by and developing Schmitz's system is Gernot Böhme (1937–2022). His interest in atmosphere started in the 1990s when he took the concept from Schmitz's new phenomenology but instead formulated his view of atmosphere in the context of a new aesthetics. The books that focus on atmosphere are *Atmosphäre: Essays zur neuen Ästhetik* (1995), *Aisthetik* (2001) and *Architektur und Atmosphäre* (2006).[19] Böhme is mentioned on several occasions by Schmitz himself as someone who has been insightfully inspired by the concept of atmosphere in *Der Gefühlsraum,* although Schmitz is sceptical of some of his modifications of it.[20] Böhme is probably the one who succeeded in making the new concept of atmosphere productive even beyond the boundaries of phenomenology, thanks to his recurrent expositions on the term in concrete and practical contexts. A not entirely unfair characterisation of the difference between Schmitz's and Böhme's way of working is that where the former mostly uses concrete examples to understand atmosphere – for example, an exposition of Homer's *Illiad* – the latter uses the concept of atmosphere also to analyse concrete objects – for example, architecture.

What is it in Böhme's use of the concept of atmosphere that Schmitz is sceptical about, and what are the substantive differences between Schmitz's new phenomenology and Böhme's new aesthetics? To answer these questions and at the same time present Böhme's understanding of the concept of atmosphere, it is first important to understand that "new aesthetics" is not a competitor of "new phenomenology" but, rather, an understanding of aesthetics inspired by the new phenomenology. Böhme sometimes chooses to speak of *Aisthetik* instead of new aesthetics to emphasise the difference with traditional aesthetics.[21] *Aisthetik* comes from the Greek *aisthesis*, meaning sensation, and is a study of the senses (our common term "aesthetics" has the same root, of course). What distinguishes *Aiestetik* from aesthetics is simply that Böhme wants to go back to a more original understanding of aesthetics, which we find in places such as the work of eighteenth-century German philosopher Alexander Gottlieb Baumgarten (1714–1762).

---

19   Böhme 2019a; Böhme 2001; Böhme 2013.
20   Schmitz 2016, p. 10; Schmitz 2003, p. vii; on Schmitz skepticism, see Schmitz 2003, pp. 243–261.
21   See, above all, Böhme 2001, pp. 11–27.

For Baumgarten, who founded aesthetics as a philosophical discipline alongside logic, it was not primarily a study of art but a study of sensory perception in general. As Baumgarten himself writes, "The goal of aesthetics is the perfection of sensory knowledge as such. This, however, is beauty."[22] The aesthetic discipline after Baumgarten has increasingly come to be about art, the artwork and artistic practice, but Böhme wants to return to this earlier, broader understanding of aesthetics as sensory perception to also include other forms of aesthetic perception that fall outside the focus on art. How do we perceive nature? What is the aesthetic status of what we call design, the aesthetics of everyday life in all its sensory and material diversity? Furthermore, aesthetics must also be broadened in relation to its traditional interest in the beautiful, the sublime and perhaps also the picturesque, Böhme argues; these can be understood as atmospheres, but aesthetic interest cannot be restricted to these atmospheres alone. This new aesthetics not only widens the field; it also gives aesthetics as such a greater critical potential in that it can address the contemporary aestheticisation of society, the idea that our lives and everything that surrounds them increasingly become a matter of staging.[23] We are in a new baroque, Böhme argues, a theatrical age, and there are reasons to understand this from a critical perspective.

The overall theme of the aesthetics advocated by Böhme is thus not art criticism but rather what he calls aesthetic labour, the production of atmospheres. Art is a particular form of aesthetic labour but only one among many, and aesthetics should therefore be concerned with the design of our entire world, from the floral wallpaper on our walls to the design of commuter trains. In modern society we have several professions working in this field: interior designers, clothing designers, scenographers and those involved in producing specific atmospheres in department stores and other environments, for example. All of the workers in these areas have practical knowledge of how to produce atmospheres, atmospheres that envelop us and move us, but the theoretical understanding of this production has been left behind. Böhme argues that this is where aesthetics finds its task. It has a critical task that is dual in nature, one could say, namely to criticise an "aesthetic pride" that is only interested in higher art and forgets the aesthetics of everyday life, but also to provide insights that make it possible to take a critical approach to the aestheticisation of everyday life.[24]

---

22    Baumgarten 2007, § 14; cf. Grote 2017, pp. 102–146.
23    Böhme 2016.
24    Böhme 2019a, p. 42.

As far as the concept of atmosphere is concerned, Böhme draws his understanding from Schmitz but, interestingly, also from Walter Benjamin, who in his famous 1936 essay on the work of art in the age of technical reproduction uses the term "aura" to refer to the bodily affective presence of the work of art (and nature) in the viewer.[25] However, the aura has hardly disappeared, as Benjamin surmised would be the case when reproductions replace the original. On the contrary, our time has become increasingly adept at producing atmospheres by utilising the aura of things.

Here we find the reason for Böhme's critique of Schmitz, on which he otherwise builds, namely that he may be strong on the aesthetics of reception – the way in which atmospheres grip us – but weak on the aesthetics of production – our production of them through aesthetic labour.[26] For Böhme, atmospheres are closely linked to things, and therefore it is also possible to produce atmospheres by organising things and ourselves in relation to each other, as interior designers, stage designers and others already do. Here we also find the reason for Schmitz's scepticism about aspects of Böhme's atmospherology – Schmitz maintains that atmospheres cannot be produced – and also the concrete difference between Böhme's and Schmitz's concepts of atmosphere. The difference is interesting in principle and in practice, and I will have occasion to return to it. In conclusion, I would just like to note that it is probably the turn to aesthetics that has both brought Böhme's atmospheric phenomenology greater attention and given it its critical potential. The critical insights into the aesthetic labour that his reflection on atmospheres gives rise to can of course function in two ways: they can be used to learn how to produce atmospheres as well as to be critical of the results of this work.

Both Schmitz and Böhme can be regarded as pioneers in phenomenological work on atmospheres. After them, it becomes more difficult to make a representative selection. However, the Italian aesthetics professor Tonino Griffero (1958–), who in a number of his own books discusses the concept of atmosphere in Schmitz and Böhme and also places it in a broad philosophical context, should be mentioned.[27] One of his main concerns has been to present a more critical conceptualization of atmosphere that contributes to the cultivation of a deeper atmospheric competence, both in terms of assessing and relating to atmospheres. However, Griffero has not only broadened the discourse on the concept of atmosphere but has also

---

25    Benjamin 1977, pp. 136–169.
26    Böhme 2019a, p. 31.
27    See, above all, Griffero 2013; Griffero 2020; Griffero 2021.

been active in communicating atmospheric phenomenology in Italian and English through translations, book series and a blog, "Atmospheric Spaces", which tries to keep up to date with what is happening in the field.[28] Griffero is mentioned by Schmitz as someone who was inspired by him, and Griffero also wrote the preface to the English edition of Schmitz's book *Neue Phänomenologie – New Phenomenology.*[29]

Griffero is himself a philosopher working largely within the phenomenological tradition. However, his focus on aesthetics (in Böhme's sense) has meant that he is also situated in the recently developing multidisciplinary and international academic dialogue on atmospheres, in which atmospheric phenomenology, previously formulated primarily within German-language phenomenology, has now reached beyond both language and disciplinary boundaries.[30] Atmospherology has proved productive in a variety of academic disciplines from psychiatry, philosophy of religion and theology to human geography, art education and theatre studies.[31] Griffero is one important but hardly the only driving force in this atmospheric field – if one can call it that – but he exemplifies well how atmospheric phenomenology, after an initiation phase with Schmitz and an establishment phase with Böhme, has now entered what we can call a dissemination phase. Atmosphere has established itself as a widely used and reasonably stable, albeit controversial, concept more broadly in academic theory. However, at least as interesting as the concept is the phenomenon it helps us to articulate. What is an atmosphere?

## Atmosphere as a Phenomenon

The starting point for answering the question of what an atmosphere is must be that there is no single atmosphere but many different atmospheres. As we have already seen, atmospheres can be peaceful, romantic or uncanny.

---

28     https://atmosphericspaces.wordpress.com (231121).

29     Schmitz 2016, p. 10; Schmitz 2019e.

30     See, for example, the seminar on architecture and atmosphere that was arranged by the Tapio Wirkkala Rut Bryk Foundation and the Alvar Aalto Academy in Helsinki in 2014, where Griffero and Böhme spoke, together with the French sociologist and urban planner Jean-Paul Thibaud and the Finnish architect Juhani Pallasmaa. See the conference volume Tidwell 2014, with contributions from Gernot Böhme, Tonino Griffero, Jean-Paul Thibaud and Juhani Pallasmaa.

31     See, for example, Costa, Carmenates, Madeira, Stanghellini 2014, pp. 351–357; Wolf 2017; Huizing 2022; Hasse 2015; Rauh 2012; Fischer-Lichte 2008, pp. 114–120.

They can be found in the Sahara, in New York City and in the houses along Mühlweg in Friedberg, or in nature, the city and the home. We have also learnt that we experience them with our bodies, that is, with all our senses, because they surround us. They therefore constitute a kind of grounding for our existence, and only secondarily do they become the object of our reflection philosophically, as in the case of the phenomenologists, or simply by formulating and talking about them in our everyday language. Atmospheres exist in some sense beyond subjective and objective. Still, we arrive at the question, what kind of phenomena are atmospheres? Is it even possible to ask such a question about them, given their elusive nature?

One way of categorising atmospheres can be found in Böhme's distinction between atmospheres and the atmospheric.[32] These differ mainly in terms of their relative distance or proximity to the self. The atmospheric is at a greater distance from the self. It can be things like night, autumn, light or wind. Some of the literary atmospheres already mentioned are, thus, examples of the atmospheric rather than atmospheres: the desert, twilight, fog. These natural phenomena are atmospheric in the way that they fill the room and thus can also affect our mood. There is an intransigence, a strangeness, to the atmospheric, against which human intentions are at odds. The atmospheric aspect of these natural phenomena can be found in the more or less everyday experience of them; in other words, it is not something that can be grasped from a perspective outside the world of human life.[33] Therefore, a scientific understanding of natural phenomena is not what is required.

The wind, for example, is not, from a phenomenological perspective, just air that moves when it blows; it is an atmospheric force.[34] It is, we might say, not only a resource from which we can extract energy through wind turbines but also an atmosphere that puts us in a certain mood, sometimes calm, sometimes a state of eagerness or tense anticipation. Both Gothenburg and Chicago are windy cities, which contributes not only to their climates but also to their atmospheres. A calm breeze on a spring evening on the shores of the North Sea or Lake Michigan might make us want to stop for a while, or it might arouse a sense of longing, while a stiff gale is more likely to activate our vigilance: is there a danger of drowning, falling trees or flying roof tiles? A much more multifaceted interpretation of wind as an atmospheric phenomenon is, of course, possible, an interpretation

---

32    Böhme 2001, p. 46. Cf. pp. 46–71.
33    Husserl 1996.
34    See Griffero 2013, pp. 13–24; cf. Bachelard 1994.

that also takes into account a culture-dependent atmospheric habit: what might be called windy in Uppland in central Sweden may be perceived as a light breeze on the Swedish West Coast. Here the wind only serves as an example of the atmospheric. The wind blows wherever it wants, without regard for human desires, even as an atmospheric phenomenon, and therefore it exists at some distance from the self. To speak of the will of the wind is, of course, a form of personification, and although the wind is not a personal partner, it is not inappropriate to liken the relationship between wind and human beings to an (unequal) partnership.[35]

The examples of the atmospheric I have mentioned are all taken from the realm of nature. As such, they can be said to form a bridge between atmospheres in the meteorological sense and in the phenomenological sense. The weather as well as the seasons affect our moods as human beings, perhaps more than ever now, at a time when nature is increasingly under human domination, and because we cannot yet control it. In art, the atmosphericity of nature is not infrequently used as a means of evoking moods in us, as we have already seen in some of my literary examples but as is also the case with the visual arts and music. An almost too obvious example of the latter is Vivaldi's *The Four Seasons*; the different ways in which the wind blows provide the music with different emotional qualities depending on the season. However, the atmospheric need not be limited to natural phenomena. It can also be a gaze, a human voice or a buzz that fills the room, as long as it is experienced as a directed, touching force and not just a physical or acoustic phenomenon.

Atmospheres, to turn now to the second part of Böhme's distinction, exist closer to the self. Atmospheres depend on a subjective reception in order not to cease to exist. In other words, we are their co-producers, if not their cause. As previously mentioned, the wind blows wherever it wants without us having any say in the matter, but the melancholy that may be in the air is not in the same way independent of our experience of it. The difference between the atmospheric and atmospheres is rather a difference of degree, where the atmospheric in the wind can give rise to an atmosphere. But if it is the case that the atmospheric is further away from the self and atmospheres closer, does it really make sense to talk about atmosphere as something that exists at least to some extent outside the self? Indeed, the common understanding of emotions in our time is that they belong to our interior.[36] I mentioned earlier that Schmitz emphatically

---

35  Schmitz 2019d, p. 127.
36  For an overview, see Hartmann 2010.

claims that emotions – at least some of them – are not internal states but in some sense external forces. Is this really true?

There are two typical experiences that suggest this is the case.[37] The first we can call the experience of entry. I sit down at a seat in the library to read, and an atmosphere of diligence and concentration envelops me. I arrive at the home of some friends after a long journey and am filled with the relaxed atmosphere. I enter the Gothic cathedral, the Victorian railway station or the packed football stadium and am struck by the room's atmosphere of reverence, of anticipation or of intensity. I enter a ceremonial hall and am struck by its festive atmosphere. All these forms of entry expose me to the atmosphere that dominates the room in question and that meets me on entry. I don't first have to be filled with devotion to be overwhelmed by the space of the Gothic cathedral, nor do I have to be in a festive mood to be struck by the festive atmosphere of the Great Hall. It is the rooms themselves that are "tuned", to use an expression we have already encountered, and so we, too, are tuned because they tune us. The fact that we can also talk in a linguistically unproblematic way, at least in Swedish and German, about how an atmosphere "possesses" the room and thus turn atmospheres into subjects further illustrates this phenomenon. The experience of entry is an experience in which I encounter the atmosphere as an object of my sensation and in which the atmosphere prompts or invites me in a certain way.

The difference between me and the atmosphere, which is a prerequisite for such an invitation, is further emphasised in what might be called an experience of discrepancy. It is also here that the difference becomes clearly visible to me. In the experience of entry, I can become so absorbed in the atmosphere that I do not notice it. A discrepancy experience is when I enter an atmosphere that differs from the mood I find myself in. This can be the experience of personal grief on a beautiful spring day, where the difference between mood and atmosphere can seem almost ironic. Or, on the contrary, entering a house of mourning in a good mood creates a discrepancy experience. I can be indifferent where others are engaged in a football match, and I can be serious among the revellers at a comedy show. Or, to refer to one of the examples of the experience of entry, the ceremonial hall does not necessarily put me in a festive mood but can also accentuate a sense of lack of cultural capital, the feeling that I don't belong there. The experience of discrepancy is about how I experience a certain

---

37    Böhme 2001, pp. 46–47.

atmosphere in spite of my own mood, and it also allows me to notice the difference between myself and the atmosphere.

The relationship between experiences of entry and of discrepancy appears to be unfixed in any given situation, in that one person's experience of a party atmosphere may be another's reminder of class. However, although our experiences of atmospheres are influenced by our personal history and social class and thus can be both supported and restrained by our habits, both of these typical experiences show that atmospheres are experienced as in some sense external forces, not just projections of our own moods onto the outside world. I meet the atmosphere as an affective touch that affects me or that I must at least relate to. To these two typical experiences, we can also add Böhme's observation that if every theatre-goer were to experience something that belongs only to the spectator's interior, stage design and the skills of the stage designer would be meaningless.[38] Traditionally, the task of the set designer is to ensure that we theatre-goers can quickly identify the atmosphere of the stage through the interplay of set, props, actors and action.

As every football fan knows, every stadium has its unique atmosphere, an atmosphere that depends on history and commitment but also on architecture. In *Crowds: Das Stadion als Ritual von Intensität*, literary scholar and football fan Hans Ulrich Gumbrecht discusses legendary stadiums such as La Bombonera in Buenos Aires, Boca Junior's home stadium, but also the Westfalenstadion, Borussia Dortmund's home stadium.[39] The latter is particularly well known for its "yellow wall", which has a standing capacity of 25,000 out of a total capacity of 80,000. The Westfalenstadion is Germany's largest stadium and is almost always full. Gumbrecht compares it to Stanford University's college football stadium, derisively referred to as "the library" because it is so quiet and rarely full. Even someone who only occasionally attends a football game will recognise the difference in atmosphere between the packed stadium and the less crowded one.

But atmosphere is not just about how many spectators are at a match. In my own hometown, there are two football arenas that are very close to each other: Gamla Ullevi ("Old Ullevi", which was actually the most recently built) and Nya Ullevi [New Ullevi]. In Gamla Ullevi, home stadium to IFK Göteborg, the stands are (relatively) vertical, the pitch is close and the acoustics separate the inside from the outside quite significantly. The

---

38    Böhme 2019a, p. 101.
39    Gumbrecht 2020.

experience at a reasonably crowded match, around 18,000 spectators, is therefore completely different from that at the multi-sport arena Nya Ullevi, even if it would be full with more than 40,000 spectators (which rarely happens), due to its flat sloping stands and the running tracks that distance the pitch from the audience. The first time I visited Gamla Ullevi, I was amazed at the difference in atmosphere that the more football-friendly architecture made. But the difference is not all architecture. Just before the game, the home crowd sings its marching song as the players enter the pitch. Of course, things like the team's standing in the league, weather and intensity of play also affect the atmosphere and the collective feeling of intense and shared presence, which according to Gumbrecht is the essence of the football experience in the stadium. The longing for a condensed moment, when suddenly the game goes your team's way, generates much of the intensity of the experience.

In other words, atmospheres are not only location- but also situation-specific, which does not prevent the existence of similarities in atmosphere between different stadiums and between matches in the same stadium. Let us therefore look at another example. Imagine the following: you pass the security and ticket control at the Stadio Olimpico in Rome as the April or October evening is turning to night. You find your seat, sit down and, after a while, find peace in the crisp, not at all unpleasant cold. The floodlights illuminate the intensely green pitch; you can smell the grass. AS Roma's players run in, the match begins, the fans scream and shoot off firecrackers and Roma wins. Together with tens of thousands of strangers, you stand up and join in Antonello Venditti's *Grazie Roma*, stumbling because you only know the words of the chorus. What do you experience? Atmosphere.

If the football stadium can be said to be an example of an atmosphere of intensity, and this intensity is something that grips you as a visiting football supporter, what happens – as a colleague of mine objected – if for some reason you come to Gamla Ullevi on match day genuinely uninterested in football? The answer is simply that this is an experience of discrepancy: my athletics-minded colleague Wilhelm would probably register the atmosphere but as something that doesn't really concern him. With a little empathy, he could realise that this is a similar experience to the one he (perhaps) has at a major athletics event. The experience of the football stadium's atmosphere is not necessarily one that forces itself on us, although as a football supporter it may be more difficult to resist. I myself am easily carried away by the atmosphere, even when I attend football matches where my own team is not playing; there is something in the situation itself that engages me. In other words, the impact of atmospheres can vary in strength depending on the situation as well as the person, ranging from a more powerful, sometimes almost unavoidable impact to a lighter appeal. They can be both brutal and subtle in their effect. However, the effect of the atmospheres is always that of a personal address: they are addressed to *me,* not to an "I" in general.

The example of the football stadium highlights an essential feature of atmospheres: although they are external to the person they surround and who is affected by them, their existence does not seem to be independent of the person they affect, which is the crucial difference between the atmospheric and atmospheres. According to phenomenologists, atmospheres exist, as we have seen, *between* subject and object. But what does this "between" mean? Böhme emphasises that one should not think of atmospheres as something completely free-floating, but at the same time they cannot be reduced to a property of things. At the same time, they are also not, as mentioned, purely subjective. Atmospheres, according to a definition by Böhme, are that which exists between the human condition and its environment in several different senses: "The atmospheres are precisely this *and*, this between both, that through which the qualities of the environment and the condition are related to each other."[40] The environment consists of objects, other people and specific events, just like at the football match, and not just things, and our state denotes how we sense this environment as something that moves us, engages us and touches us in the first person as bodily beings (as with football fans). As corporeal beings, we are necessarily in a specific place – for example, Gamla Ullevi and not Nya Ullevi – and we are in a certain way – excited about the match or not – and these factors do not create a neutral perception of the environment. As bodily beings, we are always already existentially and affectively engaged in our situation, though, as my athletic colleague made clear, not necessarily in football. A detached and analytical gaze is always secondary.

In Böhme's definition, there are three shades of this intermediate state: not only "*and*" but also "between" and "through". To begin with, the italicisation of "*and*" draws attention to the fact that atmospheres exist between our environment and our state even when they are not in focus, and this is probably their usual condition. Atmospheres are often anonymous in the sense that they are not subject to direct reflection but are assumed as some kind of horizon or mode. The purely atmosphere-less space is an abstraction. Furthermore, "between" signals how the environment and

---

40    Böhme 2019a, p. 23. I here follow the exposition of this quote in Rauh 2012, pp. 88–100.

our state exist *with* each other and not just alongside each other, as if they were independent of each other. All the objects, other people and specific events that make up a football match at Gamla Ullevi, with its particular environment, will not be an atmosphere for me if I am not also there but watching the match on TV. Finally, "through" suggests that atmospheres are the condition of this relationship. The latter means that it is *in the atmospheres* that the relationship between state and environment takes place; they are, Böhme writes, "not something relational, but the relation itself" or "the impulse to a *common* state for subject and object".[41] It should be noted that states are to be understood as something dynamic, something constantly alive, and not as a static relationship.

In other words, atmospheres are both an *interaction* between our states and our surroundings – I can sense the atmosphere of a specific football match when I am actually in Gamla Ullevi – and the *medium* through which the relationship between state and surroundings takes place – it is through the atmosphere of Gamla Ullevi that I experience the football match and myself at the football match. There is a third factor between state and environment that arises from the interaction, but also a third factor that is a precondition for the relationship between state and environment. The latter suggests that atmospheres have a kind of quasi-objective status: it is against the background of and in atmospheres that the encounter between state and environment takes place and that we experience it as an encounter. In a sense, then, it is only possible to speak of atmospheres because they precede both our state and our environment. Here our pronouns are "adverbialized" in relation to the atmospheres.[42] But at the same time, the atmospheres presuppose the interaction between our state and the environment, the concrete presence of these in each other, in order to take place. Here we also find the reason why it is possible to talk about a melancholic fog or a peaceful garden or something similar. We can speak of a fog as melancholic not because the melancholic fog resembles a melancholic person but because its atmosphericity can put a person in a melancholic mood.[43] In other words, it is the synthesising function of the atmosphere, that it constitutes this aforementioned *and*, that makes it legitimate to speak of a melancholic fog. Claiming that atmospheres have a certain character means sensing the way in which something is present

---

41    Böhme 2001, p. 54, 56.
42    Griffero 2013, p. 37.
43    Böhme 2019a, p. 34.

in someone, such as that the fog is present in a melancholic way for us by giving us a melancholic impression, or that the peaceful gardens calm us.

Thus, atmospheres are quasi-objective. What does this mean? Well, first, we can talk about them with each other and also make each other aware of what kind of atmosphere we experience, even when one of us is not affected by it. In part, this understanding is based on learning: to experience a theatre performance in much the same way, for example, to recognise a Harlequin by his costume in a classic *commedia dell'arte,* we as an audience must have been socialised into relevant genre expectations, cultural associations, among other factors. But at the same time, the reality of atmospheres can always surpass our acquired expectations in that they surprise us and will more or less abruptly retune our previous mood. The fact that we may need to actively learn what characterises a certain atmosphere and thus, in some sense, acquire a certain atmospheric competence does not contradict the fact that atmospheres have a certain quasi-objective status. We have already seen that atmospheric natural phenomena such as wind, twilight and fog are some of the objective aspects; atmospheres cannot be understood without looking at their objective properties, too. The very idea of a phenomenology of atmospheres is based on the idea that there are atmospheres with sufficiently stable characters, which are also collectively shared experiences, to make it possible to talk about them in a way that is not only emotive but also cognitive. It is not just a question of what we feel when we stand *in front of* the atmosphere, but also, to some extent, *of* the feeling as a description of it. It is true that the nature of atmospheres is that they touch us affectively, but this affective touching of us is also a touching of something that is experienced as coming from the outside and whose nature is stable enough to be articulated to some extent, at least in retrospect.

In the new phenomenology, this quasi-objective status of atmospheres has been denoted by referring to them as quasi-things or half things.[44] Speaking of atmospheres as quasi-things implies a clear break with an understanding of existence that counts only mental states and things extended in physical space or that limits existence to only one of these. Instead, the new phenomenologists advocate for a more multifaceted ontological inventory. Quasi-things exist as pure phenomena and not as physical or mental entities independent of the way they appear, unlike more solid things. According to Griffero, "the quasi-things coincide completely with the 'character' of

---

44    Schmitz 2019d, pp. 116–139; cf. Böhme 2001, pp. 61–63; Griffero 2013.

their appearance".[45] For example, the wind is blowing, but without this blowing it would be nothing; therefore, when the blowing ceases, the wind also ceases.[46] In other words, *what* quasi-things are coincides with *how* they appear, and their volatility and vagueness compared to more solid things is thus part of their essence. The point of this whole discussion of half-things is to avoid reducing the quasi-objective status of atmospheres in everyday experience to something subjective, and instead to recognise the legitimacy of these phenomena and account for it philosophically. In short, atmospheres cannot be thought away but possess a certain solidity or inertia independent of ourselves, which, moreover, persistently affect us in a way that is not entirely up to us and from which we cannot distance ourselves without them disappearing. Put another way, they are not an object among other objects but an inescapable mode through which we experience the world.

Finally, let us turn to the question of how we recognise atmospheres. It is crucial here that atmospheres as I speak of them are not first and foremost the objects of detached observation or judgement, nor the results of mental speculation. We become aware of atmospheres by being affectively touched by them in our bodily sensations. We are engaged by them and involved in them. They somehow have initiative in relation to us. Although it is possible to produce atmospheres – as I have already mentioned and will discuss more in the next chapter – the fundamental relationship to atmospheres is receptive. We are the recipients of atmospheres, which means that we are passive towards them. They claim us. However, the passivity is not absolute but rather a kind of "mediopassivity", a subject position in which we can relate actively to them only on the basis of having received their request or claim, like the tennis player returning a serve. Furthermore, the fact that the sensation is bodily means that it is a sensory perception. What sensory perception means here requires a special investigation, since the corporeality of the human being concerns both the body that lives and experiences and the body as a physical object, equipped with sense organs. Moreover, these two aspects are intertwined, as when our hairs stand up because we are facing a terrifying lion or when we get goosebumps from hearing good music.[47]

The fact that the bodily perception of atmospheres is sensory does not mean that we perceive them through a certain, individual sensory organ or

---

45   Griffero 2013, p. 17.
46   This way of putting it is borrowed from Albert Grote and found in Schmitz 2019d, pp. 117–118.
47   Böhme 2019b, especially pp. 50–60, 178–191.

that we arrange all individual sensory impressions next to each other. To give an account of what we see, hear, smell, touch or taste is to have already begun to analyse what we perceive. We are then on the way to forming a judgement about what we experience.[48] Such an analysis is, of course, part of the everyday experience of atmospheres; talking about them and trying to understand them is part of the experience itself. This is exactly what I have done above when I wanted to describe the particular atmosphere of a football stadium. But when we enter an atmosphere, we cannot differentiate between different sense impressions; atmospheres do not in themselves possess such channel specificity that they present themselves first and foremost to individual senses. Instead, they have a synesthetic character. Synesthesia usually refers to a fairly common neurological function variation where one hears colours or sees sounds, but in this context it refers to a more fundamental phenomenon: the basic sense of existence or being physically present in the world around us. Here we take in the world we are a part of as it presents itself to us through atmospheres. We also perceive our bodily presence in the room as the room's presence in and through our physicality.[49] This kind of perception can be distinguished from the perception of sensory impressions and consists of the perception of *how* we are present in the room or *what* the room means to us, that is, its affective mood: oppressive, uplifting, limiting, stifling and so on.

In other words, we find ourselves in a space that is not only a physical place with certain characteristics but also an atmosphere, and it is through both of these aspects that we sense what kind of space we are in. Sensory impressions are intertwined with disposition, our sense of being physically present in the room. At times, our individual senses may come to the fore, such as when we examine the football stadium we have just entered by looking at the pitch, listening to the noise of the crowd and smelling the concrete and grass; at other times, sensory impressions become a function of existence as we allow ourselves to be caught up in the atmosphere of pre-match anticipation and match intensity. In the former case, we behave with a certain distance from the world around us, allowing it to be the object of our exploration; in the latter, we allow ourselves to be invited or affected by it. In the former case, we are oriented towards the world with curiosity; in the latter, we are receptive to its atmosphere. Together these impressions – all sensory impressions, but also our bodily presence as such

---

48    A philosophical investigation of something so unusual as the epistemological aspects of the sense of taste is found in Perullo 2021.

49    See also Sigurdson 2022.

– create a synesthetic sensation of, for example, a shared, expectant mood. Atmospheres are, one might say, the link between sensory impressions and our fundamental disposition.

There is therefore a kind of immediacy in the perception of atmospheres. They are, according to Böhme, the "primary and in some sense fundamental objects" of perception.[50] The perception of all objects is indeed also indispensable, but the sensory curiosity about the world is secondary to the bodily-affective existence. First, we receive the world; then we can also explore it. It is, one might say, *in* the atmospheres that we also see, hear, smell, touch or taste. This is where things, other people and specific events present themselves. However, and this is crucial, it means that atmospheres are not an imagined reality but an experienced one. Even when we do not make them the object of our thoughts and even when our thoughts limit what we perceive of them, they constitute, albeit more or less unconsciously, the very medium of our perception. Atmospheres are entities that envelop us; they fill, or perhaps even create, space as they "make everything appear in a certain light, summarise the multiplicity of impressions in one mood".[51] The soft light of the blue hour lends a certain mood to our existence in which the contours and distances of things lose some of their clarity and solidity, like the objects in the Saint-Exupéry example that appeared more delicate in the moonlight. The annoying buzz of a mosquito somewhere in the room when we are about to sleep creates a completely different atmosphere, where our very skin goes into a state of tense alertness for an attack that could come at any time or place. Neither of these examples can be reduced to a mere visual or auditory impression with an origin that can be localised to a particular object, but they both concern our bodily presence in the world as a whole, right there and then. The individual sensory impressions are interchangeable with each other, so it is not always inappropriate to refer to muffled sounds as dark or high notes as sharp, or to associate certain colours with certain states of mind. Such cross-sensory impressions arise from the more basic synesthetic sense of atmospheres.

Atmospheres as phenomena are highly mundane but also elusive. They tune me before "me" becomes "I". They are the interface between ourselves and the world. Atmospherology aims to help us know atmospheres a little better through the concept, to teach us to live in them a little better and to

---

50    Böhme 2019a, p. 95.
51    Böhme 2019a, p. 103.

cure us of the obliviousness that comes from the endemic split between exterior and interior, an oblivion that leads us to easily ignore them, but which makes their power over us more diffuse. Atmospherology can therefore be said to be a critical philosophy in two different senses, and I will turn to what that means in the next chapter.

3.

## Living with Atmospheres

What does it mean to talk about atmospherology as a critical philosophy? We can start with an idea that I mentioned in the last chapter but didn't develop: the difference between being enveloped by atmospheres and producing atmospheres. The former is about how we experience atmospheres as enclosed by them; the latter refers to the aesthetic work done by architects, designers, scenographers and other workers. It is very much possible to produce atmospheres, for example, by decorating a shop in a way that exudes style, warmth and calm. Does this not mean that atmospheres are not natural phenomena at all but just constructs? And if they are not, is it also not possible to relate *to* them and perhaps even *criticise* them? Given the nature of atmospheres as external powers that dominate space and therefore grip us, the possibility of a critique of atmospheres certainly seems essential, not only to analyse them but also as a critique of power. There is nothing to say that a certain atmosphere must serve our human interests or our well-being. Therefore, the ability to form a judgement about the atmospheres we encounter is important.

However, I have also shown in the previous chapter how phenomenologists understand their rehabilitation of the philosophical status of atmospheres as a critique of the objectification of the world and the introjection of emotions in favour of a rehabilitation of the experiences of the life-world. They have also been sceptical of the "aesthetic pride" that forgets the aesthetics of everyday life in its concentration on the supposedly higher arts. Here, atmospherology appears *as a critique*. Furthermore, if there is such a phenomenon as atmospheres, which involves both an interaction between human beings and the world and a medium for their relationship, then the disclosure of this phenomenon is also a form of criticism. The unrecognised power over us that atmospheres could exercise would be more diffuse, more intangible and thus potentially more destructive than a recognised one. To do something about such power, we must first recognise its characteristics.

In other words, atmospherology contains two critical elements, which are not independent of each other: a critique *of* atmospheres, and atmospherology *as* a critique. I will not make an in-depth power analysis of atmospheres here; my aim is instead to show how this is possible within the framework of atmospherology.[1] By taking a closer look at both possibilities of critique, we can also learn what it means to live with atmospheres. Living *with* atmospheres means relating to them, which in turn implies the possibility of not being completely overwhelmed by them. This conceivable distance in their reception is also the prerequisite for the conscious production of atmospheres. Both critical moments are thus crucial to understanding our relationship with atmospheres.

*Critique of Atmospheres*

If the atmospheres, at least some of them, have the character of an external power, does this mean that we are completely at their mercy? It is easy to imagine examples of how the staging of atmospheres can be used for destructive purposes. During the Third Reich, aesthetics were deliberately and systematically used as a means to influence and shape people's thinking and behaviour.[2] Leni Riefenstahl's 1935 film *The Will to Power* is not only a documentary propaganda film about the National Socialist Party's congress in Nuremberg the year before but in itself an aesthetic expression, a skilful one, which has influenced directors far beyond the sympathisers of the message. It is easy to imagine, having seen it, that both the congress days themselves and the film were able to instil a nationalist and warlike atmosphere in the audience and thereby mobilise the masses. Hitler was, in the words of Schmitz, a successful "technician of impressions".[3] The examples could be multiplied, and there is nothing to say that contemporary politics would be free of such aestheticisations that give rise to destructive atmospheres in the political sense. This is especially relevant if what Böhme says is true, that our lives, both private and social, have increasingly become a matter of staging.[4] The power of advertising is great and recognised, but also the more informal power exercised in various ways by TV programmes and influencers is often about atmosphere.

---

1    I imagine the possibility of an intersectional analysis of power in the extension of my reasoning about ideology criticism in Sigurdson 2012, pp. 27–62.
2    Karlsson and Ruth 1983.
3    Schmitz 1999, pp. 335–337.
4    Böhme 2016.

The power of atmospheres is not physical, nor is it about commanding us to feel or act in a certain way.[5] It is more subtle in its effect. It concerns our very existence, our bodily presence in the world, our mood and our emotions. This means that although atmosphere is of course related to our senses, it is in some ways invisible and can therefore be easily manipulated. As I mentioned, it's easy to get carried away with football, at least for some of us. But what's to say that we won't get carried away in other contexts where the atmosphere is less obvious? The power through which atmospheres operate can be described as a kind of request of lesser or greater strength. It seduces rather than compels. Like Böhme, striving for greater insight into the practical knowledge of stage designers and others in their aesthetic work is therefore about learning how atmospheres function in order to enable critical judgement.

The phenomenological question of a critique of atmospheres in this sense has been raised by Böhme when he argues that Schmitz understands atmospheres too much as independent powers and is only secondarily concerned with how things are organised and how we relate to them.[6] In fact, through the staging of things and people in relation to each other, it is possible to produce atmospheres. This does not mean that Böhme gives up the quasi-autonomy of atmospheres but that he assumes a greater possibility for humans to actively relate to them. Schmitz has objected to what Böhme calls "aesthetic labour" but he himself calls "technique of impression".[7] However, significantly, he does not mention the critical potential of Böhme's aesthetics of production in this context. Only of quite late has Schmitz recognised that there may have been an earlier over-emphasis on the independence of atmospheres on his part.[8]

Griffero, on the other hand, clearly distinguishes between three types of atmospheres: prototypical, derived and inauthentic atmospheres. The difference between them is that prototypical atmospheres are "objective, external and non-intentional", derivative atmospheres are "objective, external and intentionally produced", while inauthentic atmospheres are "subjective and projected".[9] This means that the latter are not atmospheres at all but idiosyncratic feelings that we project onto something external. That all atmospheres are not projections does not exclude, for Griffero,

---

5 Böhme 2019a, p. 39.
6 Böhme 2019a, pp. 31–32. Böhme refers to Schmitz 2019a, p. 626. See also Böhme 2008.
7 Schmitz 2003, pp. 243–261.
8 See Schmitz 2016, p. 9.
9 Griffero 2013, p. 40; Griffero 2021, pp. 88–105.

that some atmospheres are indeed projections. The difference between the prototypical and the derived ones is the difference between Schmitz's more autonomous atmospheres and those that, according to Böhme, are possible to produce. Or to put it another way, it is the difference between those that have absolute authority and those with authority that is only relative. As Griffero points out, the production of atmospheres is not an exact science either. There are times when the atmosphere produced is not at all the desired one, such as when an office environment is supposed to produce an atmosphere of spontaneous and mutual exchange of ideas but instead increases stress and encroaches on the need for privacy.[10] Griffero's three types are on an affective continuum, ranging from emotional association with the atmosphere to neutral distancing.

Such a typologisation as Griffero's suggests is important for the critique of atmospheres because it shows the possibility of at least some (critical) distance to the atmospheres. The fact that it is possible to distinguish between prototypical and derived or false atmospheres does not necessarily mean that it is possible to distance oneself from atmospheres altogether. Rather, it is about being able to relate reflexively to them in the same way that it is possible to relate reflexively to one's own lived body: although I necessarily exist "here and now", it is always possible for me to relate to this "here and now" in a cognitive act that does not coincide with this positionality.[11] Certainly I am writing this here and now, but I can always relate to this writing as something external. In other words, the possible distance from atmospheres is always relative insofar as it is an attitude towards them that must be established as such.

Böhme argues that we experience atmospheres in the first person and speak of them in the third person.[12] In the first person, I am someone who is affectively affected by the atmospheres, while a third-person self, which is the accepted one in philosophical and other scientific contexts, relates to them more at a distance. As a typology, the comparison is helpful, but from a phenomenological perspective it appears somewhat exaggerated. Given that atmospheres can be conveyed through words, it is conceivable that the atmosphere you and I share is actually enhanced by exchanging a few words about it. The realisation that you are also experiencing what I am experiencing may make my experience more intense. We constantly oscillate between meaning and presence, as Hans Ulrich Gumbrecht would say.[13]

---

10    Griffero 2010, pp. 153–154.
11    See, above all, Plessner 1975, pp. 291–294.
12    Böhme 2001, pp. 50–51.
13    Gumbrecht 2004, p. 105.

The atmospherologists' perspective is essentially the same as Søren Kierkegaard's when he chastises the scholars and professors of his time for neglecting the fact that they themselves always exist in the first person and not just the third person. From their ivory towers, they suppose they can study the world from outside of it, except once a month when they collect their salary, or they think they can explain everything about love, but have themselves never loved. They "explain the whole of existence" but have forgotten their own names and that they are human beings.[14] But like Kierkegaard's reflection on existence, the atmosphericists' reflection on atmospheres also involves a relationship with them. Their books and articles are not primarily atmospheric but can be described as a movement between examples drawn from their own first-hand experience, literary, philosophical or everyday examples as well as detailed analyses of these.[15] This means that they devote themselves to describing atmospheres, including their epistemological and ontological status, from an almost purely third-person perspective. The fact that they also attribute a quasi-objective status to atmospheres ensures that it is possible to relate to them with a certain distance. Thus, if it is not only possible but also legitimate to adopt such a perspective on the atmospheres, then it is also possible to achieve a sufficient distance to be able to criticise them. However, this distance is never complete. It seems just as impossible to completely free oneself from the manipulative potential of advertising, for example, as it would be undesirable never to be surprised or overwhelmed by love.[16] Both assume that we humans are open to the world and therefore passively receiving, not just actively producing and protecting our borders.

If no absolute distance from the atmospheres is possible, what remains is a critically trained judgement, an ability to discern between spirits.[17] The capacity for judgement presupposes a sufficient distance to be able to weigh the pros and cons on the basis of certain principles of what constitutes a dignified human life, but it is not an absolute distance.[18] It is a modulation of the relationship rather than its removal. Thus, knowledge is a form of participation. It is the judgement trained when we cultivate an atmospheric competence through experience and reflection. Atmospheric competence consists of at least two different dimensions: first, to understand as far as possible how atmospheres are generated or produced; and second, to be

---

14   Kierkegaard 1991, p. 120.
15   See, for instance, Böhme 1998.
16   Griffero 2021, pp. 18, 170.
17   Cf. 1 Cor. 12:10.
18   See Sigurdson 2001, pp. 87–107.

able to open oneself emotionally to atmospheres – especially if one does not expect their existence – and thus to get to know them in order to eventually distance oneself from them. The solution is not to abandon atmospheres, if that were possible, but to relate to them in a way that combines, at least over time, affective contact and distance. The atmospherically competent can make use of the fact that there are many atmospheres and not just one, and they can play an oppressive atmosphere against a liberating one. Sometimes it can be as simple as changing rooms. It becomes more intense and challenging when an atmosphere of antagonism spreads between two groups of fans at a football match and must be broken by an atmosphere of interpersonal solidarity around football itself. The reification of the world and the introjection of emotions that characterises contemporary dualism relegates the problems of atmospheres either to the exterior or to the interior and counteracts atmospheric competence. But a human being is not by nature a neutral observer, even of atmospheres, and we must therefore learn to live with them rather than displace them.

## *Atmospherology as Critique*

For any criticism of atmospheres to be possible at all, we first need to get to know the atmospheres. However, in our time, atmospheres tend to be trivialised by being relegated our interior. Only if we recognise their quasi-objective status can we also explore to their power. The emphasis of atmospherology is not on the critique of the atmospheres but on the critique of their trivialisation, which is the effect of what Schmitz calls the "psychological-reductionist-introjectionist" reification of the world.[19] The reification of the world, which goes hand in hand with the internalisation of the emotions, results in a dualistic division between subject and object or between the inner and the outer. The subjective includes everything interior such as meaning and emotion, while the objective world consists only of the sum of material objects and appears semantically and affectively empty. It is this division between our inner and outer worlds that Schmitz criticises when he writes that a world without the quasi-things that the atmospheres are would be "cool, pale and boring".[20] The other phenomenologists also agree with Schmitz that the world in our everyday experience does not lack meaning or affective charge, but that these are always already intertwined

---

19    See Schmitz 2016.
20    Schmitz 2003, p. 105.

with our perception of the world. The basic experience of the world is of a world that means something to us and that we ourselves belong to and are part of. This does not mean that everything is perceived as immediately meaningful or that experiences of meaninglessness are untrue or inauthentic. But completely emptying the world of affective charge is a direct consequence of a long-standing desire to control the atmospheres and their power over us. This desire results in a quest to master the world and a suppression of the emotions that threaten to dominate us. Atmospherology is therefore a kind of cultural criticism, and its aim is to find the way back to a world of life that has a certain "colour" or "chromatic richness", says Griffero.[21] Restoring the atmospheres would "make human life richer in experience", Böhme argues.[22] It would release our knowledge from the impulse that relegates all extra-human affective powers to the interior and instead help us discover what bodily presence and bodily communication really consist of. As cultural criticism, atmospherology can also be said to be a critique of language that wants to help us expand our linguistic repertoire to talk about atmospheres and thus also live with them and produce them.

What the phenomenologists describe is a state of experiential and linguistic alienation, not only from the atmospheres but also from the world and oneself. It is therefore not surprising that atmospherology has attracted interest in psychopathology. Similar ideas about contemporary alienation have also been expressed in critical theory, including by Hartmut Rosa in his famous book *Resonanz* (2019).[23] Rosa is a sociologist, not a phenomenologist, but he refers to both Schmitz and Böhme and discusses mood and atmosphere. The focus of Rosa's interest is how the relationship between humans and the world can be understood through our experience of it. The two poles of this experience are "muteness" and "resonance". Experiencing the relationship with the world as a form of resonance means, in short, experiencing the world as alive in the sense that it responds in a way that is not merely an echo of the self. In other words, there is an unpredictability about the world that makes it inaccessible to my attempts to manipulate it according to my own will. To experience the world as mute is to experience it only as an echo of my own voice or a resource for the manipulations of my own will without any inherent meaning. Rosa demonstrates the contextual nature of the resonance relationship, which is related to the body, space, cultural and social situation, weather, age, religion

---

21    Griffero 2020, p. 39; Griffero 2013, p. 54.
22    Böhme 2013, p. 31. Cf. Böhme 2008, pp. 30, 34.
23    Rosa 2020, pp. 633–644.

and worldview. Our late-modern era is dominated by mute relationships to the world, but it is also characterised by a longing for resonance in a way that, paradoxically, threatens the existence of resonance when attempts to evoke it thus become attempts to control it.

In atmospheres we experience the kind of resonant relationship that Rosa speaks of. This is especially true of the atmospheres that Griffero calls prototypical rather than derived because the former are "objective, external and non-intentional" and therefore cannot be reduced to our interior nor our intention. We cannot produce them ourselves, but they arise spontaneously and affect us in a way that is beyond our control. This creates a living relationship with something that is not an image of ourselves. Rosa's point that the contemporary longing for resonance can paradoxically lead to increased muteness in the attempt to produce resonance in a controlled way leads to a question that will be addressed in the next chapter: can there be something inevitable or spontaneous in derived or produced atmospheres? Or do they, too, become mere echoes of ourselves, which can therefore be said to lack resonance? In any case, according to Rosa, the relationship of resonance is "the primary form of our relation to the world", while muteness is a secondary cultural and social product.[24] The world is not mute – or "cool, pale and boring", as Schmitz writes – in our basic experience of it. Therefore, when muteness is experienced as our primary and proper relationship to the world in our late-modern society's reification of it, it is a form of perceived alienation, not a realisation of the true nature of existence. Rosa's theory of our relationship to the world is therefore a critical theory in a similar sense as atmospherology. As when it seeks to rediscover the colour or expressive richness of existence, Rosa's theory aims to restore the experience of resonance in an increasingly numb world.

Another way to approach the cultural criticism of the atmospherologists is through Gumbrecht's question about a relationship to the world beyond – or perhaps rather this side of – our cognitive interpretation of it.[25] Our presence in the world is certainly in some sense mediated by our interpretation of it, but if we insist that our perception of a chair or a dog is our interpretation of the sensory impressions we have of a chair or a dog, then we have, perhaps unintentionally, assumed a crucial difference between our perception of something external (the chair or the dog) and our cognitive interpretation of that external (in our inner consciousness) *as* a chair or a dog. Instead of our perception of the chair or dog establishing

---

24    Rosa 2020, p. 747.
25    Gumbrecht 2004, pp. 142–143.

a relationship with them as something with which we share a world, a distance is established between thinking and things or people and the world. In our time, and particularly in contemporary academic reflection, such a distanced relationship to the world is dominant, according to Gumbrecht. We understand ourselves as consciousnesses located outside the world rather than bodily beings in the world. There are several reasons why such a self-understanding is dominant right now, reasons that are historical and philosophical and theological at the same time, but in any case, it means that we now view the world as if we were not part of it. A sense of no longer being present in the world has come to dominate the contemporary spirit, or what I would call here the contemporary atmosphere.

This alienation, which is active not only in thinking but also in our practices, gives rise to an (often unfulfilled) longing for presence, for communion *with* the world and not just an interpretation of it, according to Gumbrecht. Presence is, for Gumbrecht, "a feeling of our being-in-the-world, in the sense of being a part of the physical world of things".[26] But to be present with something, be it another person or a thing, is not only to be physically present but also, in Schmitz's words, to be "affectively touched" by it.[27] This is why "moments of intensity" or "rituals of intensity" as aesthetic experiences are so central to Gumbrecht, including football matches. The experience of our presence in the world is not something we produce ourselves but something that is seemingly spontaneously given to us or, in another sense of producing, "produced" by us and that we do not control. Such an experience of "the things of the world in their pre-conceptual thingness will reactivate a feeling for the bodily and for spatial dimensions of our existence".[28] In other words, Gumbrecht seeks to recapture a mediopassive and spontaneous experience of the world in an age dominated by an active and mediated relationship to the world, but not to completely replace the latter with the former.

The atmosphere of a football match (especially Borussia Dortmund's home games) is thus described by Gumbrecht as an atmosphere of intensity. Intensity is, as it were, a form of presence. The intention of Gumbrecht's previously mentioned book on football is, among other things, to show

---

26  Gumbrecht 2004, p. 116.
27  Gumbrecht rather speaks of "moments of intensity", "the specific appeal of such moments", their "typical situational framework", the "specific disposition" they demand of us, what "fascinates us" in them, about "epiphanies", even an "element of violence" and also a "loss of control" (Gumbrecht 2004, pp. 96–118), but like atmospheres, presence is quasi-objective, external and spontaneous.
28  Gumbrecht 2004, p. 118.

how football matches on TV can never replace the experience of watching football in a stadium. Football on TV is and remains ghost football because the TV broadcast cannot convey the atmosphere of the stadium, a shared experience of bodily concentration and intense presence. At the same time, we are increasingly dependent on digital media to bring the world to us. Sometimes we simply don't have the opportunity to travel to where the football match that is important to us is actually being played, or we can't get tickets, and then TV is the option we have. But he is right that digital media, like all other media, is doing something to our relationship with the world. It will therefore be interesting to conclude this discussion on atmospheres as critique by turning to digital spaces to see what kinds of presence and atmosphere they can and cannot convey and why. Can atmospherology be understood as a critique also of the proliferation of digital spaces in our time?

*Digital Spaces*

What kinds of presence or atmospheres characterise our digital spaces? Undoubtedly it involves a kind of spatiality, with all the screens that surround us and that we turn to in our contemporary everyday life: the mobile phone, the computer, the car, the billboard, the coffee machine and the arena concert, to name only a few. All of them offer a kind of visual interface between the world and ourselves. Some screens, like the billboard, are mostly a form of one-way communication. Others, like the front of the coffee machine or in the car, offer an interactivity where I can control certain functions. However, some of them, such as the computer and the mobile phone, involve a form of social interaction between two or more people. Such digital interaction can constitute a "telepresence" or "mediated immediacy", in some respects as present as a physical face-to-face meeting.[29] The mediated presence of digital space is not necessarily an inferior or subordinate version of physical space, which can be a common perception. It is easy to find examples of how the telepresence of an email correspondence, a series of text messages or simply an old-fashioned phone call can be experienced as a presence much like coexisting with someone in the same room. The digital space that is a function of digital communication technologies is today not a virtual parallel to the corporeal space of lived experience but inseparably intertwined with it; with a modicum of digital

---

29    Cf. Lindemann and Schünemann 2020, pp. 627–651.

literacy, we move almost effortlessly between the person on the mobile phone screen and the people in the room, or between the slow meeting and the (constantly postponed) promise of some crucial news in our email. The point of critically reflecting on presence in digital spaces is thus not that there must be a given qualitative difference between them and analogue spaces, or that the kind of mediated immediacy they offer can only be a poor copy of the (supposedly) unmediated immediacy of the physical meeting. The more interesting question is what kind of presence all the different spaces can offer.

In the Galleria Doria Pamphilj in Rome hangs Diego Velázquez's portrait of Pope Innocent X (circa 1650), recognised as one of the greatest painted portraits ever.[30] We find it in a small side room. The lighting is considerably muted compared to the opulent corridors around it, where work after work of the marvellous collection hangs. Apart from a Bernini bust of the same pope, the illuminated portrait is the only artwork in the dark room. Approaching this work means making it the object of one's own gaze while crossing the border between light and darkness, where attention to the position of the artwork in relation to my physical presence is heightened thanks to the clear focus of the room. I do not remain static in relation to the portrait either but move closer, taking a step to the side, moving away and then approaching again. Even if I do not touch the artwork with my fingertips, I am acutely aware of being in its presence and, in a slightly eerie way, of being in some sense the object of a gaze directed at me from the Innocent X I see depicted. In other words, the presence that I become part of in relation to a work of art of this kind is not merely a matter of visual presence. As Jean-Louis Chrétien points out, "It is not with one's eyes but rather with all one's being that one looks upon a picture."[31] The kind of attention I pay to Velázquez's portrait is also not only a question of gaze and existence; it is also about the gallery as a social space. Although I do not share the side room with any other visitor, I do so in my experience of the gallery as a whole, with other visitors, the museum staff and my general knowledge of how to behave in a museum. The museum and gallery are not only places for aesthetic contemplation but also for social interaction.[32] My presence in front of Velázquez's portrait is thus conditioned not only by the aura of the artwork in Benjamin's sense but also by the atmosphere

---

30    Gombrich 2006, pp. 311–312.
31    Chrétien 2003, p. 18.
32    Madsen 2019, pp. 229–247.

of the entire gallery. In the gallery I meet Velázquez's Innocentius X body to body.

When I later want to recall the portrait, I don't go to the gallery but to the photographs I took of the work during my visit or to a digital reproduction from the Internet. Here I am able to concentrate on details by enlarging those that interest me, and I am not stressed by the fact that other visitors may want to encounter the work of art in the same way as I do. I wouldn't say that its digital reproduction has lost all aura, but the atmosphere of the gallery and my ability to move in relation to the work is lost. Regardless of the degree of magnification, the image is displayed on the same square, flat surface, and there is really no point in moving my eyes or body since only a shift in the surface of the image on the fixed screen creates a kind of change in perspective.[33] It is also on the same (kind of) screen that I conduct my email correspondence, write this book, watch films and other images and meet students via Zoom. The multiple uses of the digital screen, together with its static nature, create a different type of presence than standing body to body with Velázquez's portrait. Galleria Doria Pamphilj is filled with a different atmosphere than my office. The difference in my attention to the artwork on the screen and in the gallery can be described, in a nutshell, as that between a meditation that I actively seek and a mediopassive and spontaneous contemplation. Whilst I can reach out my fingers to touch the portrait on the screen without consequence, the movement is now devoid of all allure. Whatever I see, there is nothing to touch but a plastic screen.

Teaching in schools and universities has increasingly come to rely on digital communication technologies for traditional lectures and seminars instead of the usual campus classrooms, a development that was accelerated by the coronavirus pandemic. It is important to explore the pedagogical implications and effects of this shift. The digital classroom differs from the tangible classroom on campus in a similar way that the digital museum differs from the tangible museum, in that everything to be communicated in the classroom is transformed to fit within the confines of the rectangular screen and its sound reproduction system. The digital platform invites a different relationship between the student and the teaching, where the student has more control than in the physical classroom. It is possible to listen and watch with concentration but also to comment, switch off the camera and remain relatively invisible to the teacher and also, more than in the physical classroom, to be distracted by what is happening on or beside the screen. The teacher, on the other hand, has a different set of

---

33    Rosa 2017, p. 25.

pedagogical tools at their disposal, as all of them have to be adapted to the digital platform and its flat, rectangular screen. This pedagogical scenario accentuates the differentiation between the teacher as producer and the student as consumer, but both become disembodied spectators or providers of information rather than embodied and engaged participants. As a result, the pedagogical situation is also privatised. Power over teaching becomes, in effect, power over digital communication technologies, with the camera and the off button as tools.

In the traditional classroom, the teacher and student not only share a classroom; they are also surrounded by a pedagogical atmosphere that is an affective condition for teaching.[34] This means both that the teaching is more interactive and multimodal – or simply bodily mediated – than in the digital classroom and that it thus also enables an atmosphere of, for example, curiosity, trust and critical exploration and not just information transmission. The affective register of teaching is broader in the physical classroom than in the digital, which presumably facilitates learning and the ability to critically engage with what is being taught. If learning is not just about collecting facts but also about forming a judgement that helps to orient oneself physically, with desires, interests and aims in the lifeworld, then the very atmosphere of the classroom is crucial to this educational process. The educational atmosphere is about the possibility of acquiring a favourable disposition for learning in general rather than about acquiring a certain amount of information.

Looking at the digital classroom versus the physical one is a matter of abstraction, as much as looking at the digital image versus the gallery portrait. The digital classroom can probably work well as a complement in blended learning environments, where telepresence can convey a presence between teachers and students as well as in other social situations. For experienced students with already established academic skills and a relationship with academic learning as such, the temporary digital classroom presents fewer problems. But as a dominant medium, it risks being characterised by muteness in Rosa's sense. An atmospheric poverty and bluntness are combined with the aforementioned privatisation of the pedagogical situation.

Thus, what is at stake in the question of presence and atmosphere in digital spaces is not whether any kind of presence is possible or not but what kind of presence it is. That digital spaces can be important elements of the broader existential space is highly probable, but more crucial are

---

34    Bollnow 2001; Dreyfus 2008.

the consequences for the atmosphere that the dominance of digital spaces could have.[35] Digital spaces are characterised by their channel specificity.[36] The ubiquitous screen undoubtedly privileges the sense of sight, which has historically been associated with human intellectual abilities and has therefore sometimes been seen as distant and almost incorporeal.[37] Although a more embodied understanding of the sense of sight is possible, the screen as the visual interface of digital space tends to create a static understanding of the relationship between human beings and the world of the kind described by the atmospherologists but also by Rosa and Gumbrecht: there is a qualitative difference between subject and object in this space. Of course, the digital space also includes the sense of hearing; our interaction with other people via the screen is often supplemented by sound. Even if contemporary digital communications have their own specific challenges, there is no fundamental difference between these and other forms of remote communication through sound reproduction, such as phone calls. However, at least in the current state of technology, the digital space is a space without smell, taste or touch. Added to this is the crucial absence of any sense of dynamic mobility and positionality in relation to someone or something else, a sense in which affective intensity and physical proximity are combined in one way or another.

The reservation about presence in digital space is not that all forms of presence are impossible but that digital space does not reach the same synesthetic richness as bodily space. Böhme argues at one point that the channel specificity of communication technologies means that the digital communication partner only appears before us as an actor on a stage.[38] However, this needs not be the case. Rather, what matters is the relationship that digital communication occupies in the person's overall lifeworld. Since no communication technology is neutral but inevitably entails a certain conception of the relationship between human beings and the world, including both individual human experience and social structures, the dominance of the digital space over the spaces where we interact body-to-body will imply some kind of reification of the communication partner.[39] However, the fact that we occasionally use the phone as a means of communicating even more intimate and personal matters with

---

35    See Lagerkvist 2022.
36    See Böhme 2013, p. 121.
37    Sigurdson 2006, pp. 151–180.
38    Böhme 2013, p. 121.
39    See Rosa above, but also Sacasas 2020, pp. 3–18, Han 2021, as well as – and not least – Kittler 1995.

someone we already have a concrete relationship with hardly means that our lifeworld is colonised by the digital space. Telepresence is indeed a form of presence with the other. Channel-specific communication can probably always complement, and in some specific cases even replace, a broader range of communication and relationality of a particular kind. The place of digital communication technologies in the lifeworld's broader ecology of communicative registers is therefore crucial also for their atmospheric meaning: do they constitute an impoverishment or expansion of the lifeworld? The channel-specific presence of digital space negates presence in general only when its specificity is allowed to dominate human existence. Neither the museum space nor the classroom can be replaced by digital space, but digital space can become part of them. The crucial question is which space is allowed to dominate, a space that lends itself to a richer or poorer presence and atmosphere?

Discussing atmospherology as a critical philosophy is about learning to live with atmospheres, not about thinking we can escape them. But learning to live with atmospheres is something we do, not only because we must but mainly because they allow us to get closer to things and the world, which can enrich life. The argumentation about atmospherology as criticism, as with Rosa and Gumbrecht, is based on a fundamental recognition of the experiences we have and make of living in the world. There are several critical questions to be asked, not only about atmospheres as such but also about atmospherology. But whatever the answer to these questions, it is important to articulate, like these phenomenologists, what kind of affirmation of the world that makes a critique possible. In other words, we must articulate what notion of the relationship between human beings and the world is at stake in both affirmation and critique.

4.

ATMOSPHERE AND ARCHITECTURE

Atmospheres surround us and urge us on. They thus appear as something beyond our control. Nevertheless, we also seem to be able to produce atmospheres through the staging of things and people in relation to each other. In relation to atmospheres, we are then not only receptive but also productive. The critical interest in atmospheres is partly conditioned by the fact that there are whole professions that possess practical skills in staging atmospheres, atmospheres that we experience as immersive and that capture us even when we realise that they are produced to do just that, such as in the theatre. Certainly, in the theatre it is possible and sometimes even necessary to have what Bertold Brecht calls *Verfremdungseffekte*, breaking the spell of the play by making it clear that the atmosphere is staged and deliberately produced. But even this negative possibility seems to presuppose that it is actually possible, and in some sense inevitable, to stage atmospheres with an affective incitement we must relate to as something other than ourselves.[1]

That architecture can be understood as a fundamental form of staging atmospheres that affect us all is a fact that has escaped neither phenomenologists nor architects. On the contrary, the reflections of atmospheric phenomenologists are full of references to architecture. Architects, on the other hand, have formulated themselves both independently of and in dialogue with phenomenology about architecture as a form of producing atmospheres. When the Swiss architect Peter Zumthor defines what for him constitutes architectural quality, he refers to the experience of being touched by the atmosphere that characterises a building.[2] He speaks of the "magic of the real" and asks whether it is possible for him, as an architect, to create qualitative atmospheres and if so, how. In other words, Zumthor's question concerns *how* atmospheres can be produced and *what* can produce them.

---

1    Fischer-Lichte 2008, pp. 114–120.
2    Zumthor 2006, pp. 11–13, 19. Cf. Zumthor 2017, pp. 83–87.

Zumthor speaks in the first person. Among phenomenologists, the claims are more general, such as Griffero's assertion that architecture "as the art of experienced and affective space" belongs at the core of atmospheric aesthetics.[3] Griffero relies on Böhme, who argues that "the work of architecture consists essentially in the creation of atmospheres".[4] There are several reasons why atmospherologists are so interested in architecture: first, architects are an example of a professional group that works concretely to produce atmospheres and therefore possesses a practical knowledge of them; second, architecture clarifies the intimate relationship between spatiality and atmosphere; and third, architecture raises questions about the experience of space, including how human physicality and sensibility should be understood in relation to it. Particularly if one formulates it as Finnish architect Juhani Pallasmaa does, that architecture is a way of confronting existential questions about human beings in time and space, it becomes clear that architects and phenomenologists share many issues, even if they approach them from different directions. Discussing atmosphere and architecture therefore becomes a way to deepen insights into atmospheres in everyday life by examining a concrete, atmospheric practice.


*The Architecture of the Eye and the Body*


From perceiving the concept of atmosphere as "banal, romantic or simply kitsch", Pallasmaa came to refer to it in 2013 as "one of the fastest spreading subjects in schools of architecture around the world".[5] He also points out that it took him 75 years to realise how central the concept was. Pallasmaa (1936–) has worked with architecture on different scales for many years but has also established himself as a theorist, with a number of books dealing with different aspects of architecture in dialogue with fiction, phenomenology, neuroscience and film. Here, Pallasmaa not only combines his experience as a practising architect with intellectual breadth but also articulates some basic questions about the human relationship with architecture: what kind of understanding is presupposed by different types of architecture? Through which senses do we relate to architecture?

---

3    Griffero 2020, p. 14.
4    Böhme 2013, p. 105.
5    Tidwell 2014, p. 67. Cf. pp. 67–70. Cf. Borch 2014, where Pallasmaa as well
     Böhme were published after speaking at the same conference in Copenhagen
     Business School May 17 2011, but also Pallasmaa 2012, p. 13.

According to Pallasmaa, the fact that the concept of atmosphere has long been a blind spot in architecture is due to modernism's scepticism about multifaceted and distinctive materiality as well as traditional building techniques, but also due to the fact that architecture has been understood above all as a visual art that strives for clarity. In fact, twentieth-century modernist architects such as Frank Lloyd Wright, Alvar Aalto and Sigurd Lewerentz consciously strived to create atmospheric architecture. Over time, it has also been understood that architecture is a multisensory rather than a purely visual art. As a result, the concept of atmosphere is close at hand.

The last reason for the return of atmospheres in architecture is also what Pallasmaa sees as the main reason. The basic critical question that he has posed to architecture, even before he became familiar with the concept of atmosphere, is formulated in the question of its oculocentrism: what does it mean to make the sense of sight the most significant sense in the experience of architecture? In Pallasmaa's most famous book *The Eyes of the Skin*, it is precisely the oculocentrism, not only in architecture but in Western culture as a whole, that is the focus of his criticism. Oculocentrism means, in short, that the human sense of sight is understood as the sense that fundamentally determines a person's relationship to the world around them.[6] This privileging of the sense of sight, which can be found throughout Western history, is not so much a biological fact as an intertwining of biology and culture, in which the gaze is understood in terms of distance, agency and control: I stand at a distance from the object I am looking at, it is I who actively strives to look at the object, which is therefore passive towards me, and I do so in order to control it. The fact that vision determines our relationship with things therefore means that we will think of ourselves as separate from the world rather than participating in it.

According to Pallasmaa, architecture is an art through which we try to understand and articulate the existential conditions of our existence. This then means that its inherent oculocentrism has consequences for how we understand our existence, as it primarily addresses the eye and the intellect.[7] Architectural theory, from Leon Batista Alberti onwards, has always emphasised an oculocentric approach to architecture, says Pallasmaa. Le Corbusier's early writings are steeped in visual metaphors, and although, according to Pallasmaa, he possessed a haptic sensibility in his sketches

---

6     On oculocentrism, see Sigurdson 2016, pp. 115–181. Pallasmaa refers above all to the standard work, Jay 1993.
7     Pallasmaa 2012, pp. 12–13, 22.

as well as in his architecture, the sense of sight came to be crucial to his work in general and his urban planning projects in particular.[8] It may be worth emphasising that Pallasmaa is not primarily interested in criticising modernism as an architectural style but, rather, the self-understanding of some of its important representatives.

What is the alternative to oculocentrism in architecture? According to Pallasmaa, it is an architecture oriented towards human physicality, where all the senses play a role and where the role of the haptic sense in particular is valued. In contrast to the distance and control of the visual sense, the sense of touch is perceived as intimate, close, and truthful; it therefore represents a conception of the human relationship with the world that is characterised by participation. Pallasmaa illustrates the multisensory nature of our bodily relationship with the world through a brief description of a city walk leading to a cathedral:

> I confront the city with my body; my legs measure the length of the arcade and the width of the square; my gaze unconsciously projects my body onto the façade of the cathedral, where it roams over the mouldings and contours, sensing the size of recesses and projections; my body weight meets the mass of the cathedral door, and my hand grasps the door pull as I enter the dark void behind.[9]

Notice that the sense of sight also plays a role in this quote but is not dominant, unlike its role in oculocentrism. By talking about how it is through the body that we encounter the city, the body mentioned in the passage above also plays an integrating role for all senses. Although Pallasmaa does not mention in the quotation the sense of smell or taste, so important to the experience of the city, he returns elsewhere to the importance of these senses, particularly in the experience of visiting a new city. In other words, the problem is not the sense of sight itself but its dominance and its exclusivity when it does not cooperate with the other senses. When the visual and haptic senses cooperate, there is no absolute distinction between sight and touch, and the former can be understood as a touch at a distance.[10] Overall, Pallasmaa's understanding of the relationship between the senses can be interpreted as synesthetic, as he repeatedly refers to them in terms

---

8    Pallasmaa 2012, p. 32. An obvious example we find in Le Corbusier 1986.
9    Pallasmaa 2012, p. 43. Cf. how Peter Zumthor describes how he enters his mothers' garden in Zumthor 2017, p. 7, and how this becomes a kind of foundational experience.
10   Pallasmaa 2012, p. 46.

of each other in a seemingly paradoxical way: "the skin of the eyes", "the thinking hand" and "the embodied image".[11] It is the exclusivity of the visual sense in oculocentrism that Pallasmaa opposes, in favour of a more multisensory approach to architecture in which the different senses also spill over into each other instead of functioning alongside each other.

What are the consequences for architecture with this alternative to oculocentrism? The starting point for understanding architecture from this perspective is that it is more about lived space than geometric space. Buildings are spaces that we humans constantly interact with rather than objects we react to; the relationship between body and space thus becomes different. It is significant that the above quote is about how Pallasmaa describes entering a building rather than looking at it from the outside. Architectural spaces serve primarily as invitations to action: to grab the handle, open the door and enter, then to be asked by the space one enters to move and act in a certain way. Thus, characteristics that invite all the senses into an exploratory interaction with the space become important. Here, Pallasmaa argues that homogenised characteristics, whether they involve touch, light or sound, tend to paralyse the imagination and make the experience of the space less vivid. Therefore, things like the choice of materials and colours, the variety of light and the acoustic design of the room become important. It is imperative that the room in question can be inhabited beyond pure functionality. For this to be possible, the room cannot be too easy to appropriate; it must also be able to offer some resistance so as not to lose its relative secrecy. The space cannot surrender itself to the exploratory gaze but should instead present itself little by little to those who are physically present in it.

Of course, different architectures emphasise different senses: the eye, but also the skin, the ears, the nose and the tongue. The decisive criterion for what Pallasmaa considers good architecture seems to be its multisensory effect. Instead of the "architecture of the eye" that is the effect of oculocentrism, Pallasmaa advocates for what he calls Aalto's "sensory realism", which he says is characterised precisely by an "agglomeration" of sensory impressions.[12] This architecture is based on craftsmanship at least as much as rational calculation and planning, as craftsmanship is practical, multisensory knowledge that is in the body and the hand, not

---

11    The two latter quotes refer to the titles of Pallasmaa 2009 and Pallasmaa 2011. Pallasmaa is, of course, not the first modernist architect that has pointed out the interdependence between eye and body. See, for example, Schwartz 1947, pp. 9–11.

12    Pallasmaa 2012, p. 76. Cf. Pallasmaa 2009, p. 15.

just in the eye and the intellect.[13] The craftsman as a type signals a different relationship to the world than the engineer as a type: craftsmanship is a bodily practice that implies a participation in the world, rather than having an instrumental relationship to it; it is a marriage between hand and head rather than a divorce, so to speak. Without craftsmanship, the intimate and sensual connection between imagination and building risks being lost.[14] Quoting Maurice Merleau-Ponty's essay on Cézanne's painting, Pallasmaa claims that "the task of architecture is 'to make visible how the world touches us'", and this motto can serve as a summary of Pallasmaa's vision of the architecture of sensory realism.[15]

Pallasmaa's critique of oculocentrism, his advocacy for a multisensory approach to architecture and his valorisation of craftsmanship as a phenomenon also shed light on what other architects have written about atmospheres. Zumthor (1943–), who is best known for a swimming pool complex in Vals, published a book in 2006 entitled *Atmosphären,* in which he argues that the task of the architect involves "an interaction between people and things".[16]

Unlike Pallasmaa, Zumthor does not refer to other authors in the field but reflects on his own experience as an architect and previously also as a cabinetmaker. The question I mentioned at the beginning, whether it is possible to produce atmospheres, he answers directly: the task of the architect is "to create architectural atmospheres".[17] When Zumthor goes on to describe how this is done, we recognise ideas from Pallasmaa: it is about bringing together materials in the world and creating spaces where these materials are allowed to resonate together. Out of this composition comes something unique, a space with a specific sound and a specific temperature (in a broad sense: physical, musical and architectural), related to these materials. In this space we move amongst the things it contains and get to know it as we move through it. The space arises in a tension between inside and outside and expresses a relationship with the people in it. Finally, atmosphere is also about how the space is lit. Zumthor sees this description of how it works, which I have tried to capture above,

---

13    Pallasmaa 2009, p. 15 *et passim*. Pallasmaa mentions on p. 5 that he is influenced by Sennett 2009. Sennett here defines craftmanship on p. 8 as "the skill of making something well" and suggests in his book that this is a combination of embodied practice and imagination.
14    Pallasmaa 2009, p. 65.
15    Pallasmaa 2012, p. 49; Maurice Merleau-Ponty 1964, p. 19.
16    Zumthor 2006, p. 17.
17    Zumthor 2006, p. 21. Cf. Zumthor 2017, p. 10.

as an idiosyncratic summary in nine points, taken from himself and his architectural office.[18] To these he adds the importance of the environment and use of architecture: how a building relates to its environment and how it is used are also important.

Zumthor thus advocates for an architecture that touches; atmosphere and affectivity are linked when architecture is allowed to be a "sensitive vessel" for basic existential activities.[19] What are these activities? They are everyday occurrences: "the rhythm of the steps on the floor", "the concentration of work", "the stillness of sleep" and countless others. The main point for Zumthor is that these everyday activities are not just instrumental. Activities like taking a few steps to get a cup of coffee, working to live or sleeping to recover are existentially significant activities, which therefore require an architecture that touches us existentially in a way that corresponds to this significance. In Pallasmaa's words, it is not an architecture of the eye that Zumthor seeks but something more multimodal.

For the Danish architect and sculptor Anders Gammelgaard Nielsen, who currently works at the Aarhus School of Architecture, atmosphere is also generated by the materiality of buildings. What makes him interesting in this context is not primarily the connection to his own practice in architecture but two theoretical questions that are at the centre of his book *Atmosfære og byggekultur/Atmosphere and Building Culture*: is it possible to convey some element of a certain atmosphere in a commentary on it? Also, can one say something about what contributes to a good atmosphere in a room?

The main body of *Atmosphere and Building Culture* is occupied by a series of observations or case studies of nine different rooms: through photographs, associative keywords and a brief, neutral description, Gammelgaard Nielsen aims to convey or evoke something about the atmosphere of each of these rooms, albeit in a different medium from the rooms themselves. The "restrained" room, which dates from the early twentieth century, is said to be "characterised by sobriety and precision", where craftsmanship has contributed a restrained elegance; in contrast, the "clinical" room is characterised by fragmentation, as the building elements do not relate to each other, and by monotony, due to the prefabricated elements and their colours without depth. The latter therefore appears "flat and boundless, inviting only a temporary stay".[20] These case studies

---

18   Zumthor 2006, p. 63.
19   Zumthor 2017, p. 12. Cf. p. 19.
20   Gammelgaard Nielsen 2021, pp. 49, 89.

cannot, of course, replace the experience of being present with the body in the concrete spaces, but they can be said to convey, through multiple presentations, both textual and visual, something of this atmosphere.

The hypothesis guiding Gammelgaard Nielsen's research is that the industrialisation of building culture has led to a homogenisation of the various architectural spaces, from schools, hospitals and daycares to offices and homes. The result is a kind of "atmospheric boredom", which does not correspond to our varied uses of these different spaces; the atmosphere of the room should actually support our everyday and diverse uses of the rooms, but this does not happen if all rooms carry the same atmosphere.[21] A standardised building culture will affect atmospheres by also standardising materials and technologies, compared to the more irregular processes of pre-industrial craft culture. If industrial standardisation is able to produce exactly the same modules and colours, the builder or painter will always leave his personal, more irregular traces through manual craftsmanship. There is therefore, at the level of detail, a greater variety in the handcrafted space, a variety that contributes to an atmosphere that is experienced as more "vibrant and saturated" than the more silent, standardised space that can tend toward a "sterile and forbidding" atmosphere.[22] The handcrafted room allows a wider range of sensory impressions to play a part in the perception, and it thus takes longer to take in the room as a whole. Even the materials themselves can contribute to or reduce the atmospheric richness of a room in their colour, the way they are processed and the way they are constructed. Natural and artificial materials therefore affect the atmosphere in different ways.

In fact, Gammelgaard Nielsen argues that the way we build largely determines the atmosphere of spaces. A way of building with more variety, as in the earlier craft culture, leads to more resonance between the room and those who are in it, while a more standardised building leads to a muter relationship between human being and room; the atmosphere is therefore more alive in the former than in the latter. This does not mean that the "living" room is always preferable to the more sterile room. The fact that a room is sterile is not a problem in itself. It only becomes a problem when the use of the room and its atmosphere differ too much. In a medical intensive care unit, the sterile room is functional for the activities carried out in it, but if our home is built in the same sterile way as the operating theatre, it will be difficult to make ourselves at home there. According to

---

21    Gammelgaard Nielsen 2021, p. 79. Jfr p. 103.
22    Gammelgaard Nielsen 2021, p. 112.

Gammelgaard Nielsen, the atmosphere should support the use of the room. The conclusion is therefore that since construction affects the atmosphere of the room being built, the variety of human life should be matched by an expanded atmospheric repertoire and therefore also by a varied construction where craftsmanship and industrial production interact with each other.

The point of Gammelgaard Nielsen is not nostalgic – that natural materials are always better than composites – but multisensory. The variety serves our sense of belonging in the room, what he in Danish calls "hjemliggørelse", the act of appropriating a room so that it becomes one's own in some sense, so that we feel "at home" there, even if it is not necessarily a home in the literal sense. In Pallasmaa's terms, we can understand Gammelgaard Nielsen's examination of the atmospheres of spaces as a critique of oculocentrism and an advocacy of multimodal architecture.

It is interesting to note how the three architects I have discussed here all emphasise the tactile and dynamic dimension of architecture. Such a synesthetic and embodied understanding of sensation, including the interdependence of the senses, has been supported by contemporary neuroscience, including Vittorio Gallese's investigation of aesthetic experience. At the biological level, the senses do not exist as separate from each other even though we talk about them this way.[23] Sarah Robinson has also pointed out that emotion and cognition have been separated in Western intellectual history in a way that has consequences for architecture and reflection on it; therefore, the haptic sense becomes important in the attempt to recover a connection between them, as it promotes closeness rather than distance.[24] She does not explicitly mention atmospheres, but Niels Albertsen does. He was among the first in the Nordic countries to point out how the concept serves to re-establish other senses in relation to the dominant oculocentrism of architecture.[25]

The architects I have mentioned thus seem to be reaching for the concept of atmosphere, a term that they probably would draw on at least as much from everyday language as from phenomenology, to express a concern that they seem to have in common: a critique of the oculocentric understanding of the relationship between human beings and space, coupled with an advocacy for a multimodal architecture that corresponds to our multisensory existence. The invocation of atmosphere in Pallasmaa and Zumthor

---

23   Se for instance Gallese 2015, pp. 64–77, but also Freedberg and Gallese 2007, pp. 197–203. Cf. also Canepa 2022.
24   Robinson 2015, pp. 43–63.
25   Se for instance Albertsen 1999, pp. 9, 11.

is not a reactive nostalgia nor an advocacy of a return to some kind of "classical" architecture. In the same breath that modernism is criticised for its oculocentrism, representatives from the same modernist canon as those being criticised are cited as examples of atmospheric architects: Aalto, Lewerentz and even, albeit with some reservations, Le Corbusier. Nor is their critique a critique of a particular style of modernism. Rather, their approach can be understood as a discussion within modernism itself of how the technological innovations in the art of building, which once gave rise to modernism, should be used in a way that does not pit industrial production against craftsmanship and instead promotes a multisensory approach to buildings.[26]

In a sense, the introduction of the concept of atmosphere in architecture can be understood in part as a proposal for a deeper self-understanding rather than a radically different building practice, though the concrete construction is, of course, dependent on how architecture understands itself. But the architecture of modernist architects might be thought to transcend even their own modernist *credo* and not just the polemical front against which it was directed. As Pallasmaa has argued, some of the most prominent modernist architects of the twentieth century, including Le Corbusier, explicitly articulated atmospheric architecture.[27] It is also reasonable to imagine, if there is anything in the criticism of the architecture of the eye that we have encountered here, that a wide range of architects have practised something similar without having articulated the matter as thoroughly. I therefore argue that the use of the concept of atmosphere by these architects is more a critique of the self-understanding of architectural practice as such than of a particular architectural style, modernist or other. Pallasmaa and Zumthor, more or less in dialogue with phenomenology, express the kind of practical knowledge that Böhme considers to be the prerequisite for the aesthetic work of producing atmospheres.


*Phenomenology of Multimodal Architecture*

Of course, the new phenomenologists were not the first to come up with the idea of a phenomenology of architecture, nor even the first phenomenologists to use atmosphere as a concept in relation to architecture. One of the most famous works of architectural phenomenology is Christian

---

26   Cf. Sharr 2018, *passim.*
27   Cf. Le Corbusier 1986, pp. 1, 4.

Norberg-Schultz's *Genius Loci: Towards a Phenomenology of Architecture* from 1980. In this book, the Norwegian architect, using an interpretation of Heidegger's thoughts on dwelling, wants to approach the existential questions through architecture in a way reminiscent of what we have seen in this chapter. *Genius Loci* is an ambitious and wide-ranging book with lots of images to accompany its thesis that a concrete place is characterised by a particular "spirit of place" and the role of architecture is to visualise this *genius loci*, thereby helping people to inhabit a place in a meaningful way.[28] The place and its concretisation through architecture becomes a shield against human existential homelessness. However, Norberg-Schultz has been criticised for the fact that his book, particularly its visual material, nevertheless pursues the oculocentrism that, according to Pallasmaa, has plagued the historical but above all the contemporary understanding of architecture.[29]

Even if Norberg-Schultz is mentioned by the new phenomenologists, there is rarely any major discussion or use of his ideas as a starting point.[30] One reason for this is probably the very oculocentrism that Norberg-Schultz's book exhibits. With explicit reference to Pallasmaa, Böhme has questioned whether architecture is a visual art that is best represented through visual media.[31] If the task of architecture is to design spaces for human activities, it is simply not pertinent to represent architecture by depicting buildings in direct, clear, and static photographs. Architectural photography, if it is to correspond to the task of architecture, must instead somehow reproduce the experience of space that we make in the building so that the experience of the photograph corresponds to the bodily experience of the space. In this latter case, the room does not become an object but rather the horizon against which different objects can appear in the room. In other words, the space Böhme discusses here is not geometric space but existential space, which is the dynamic background both to human action and to the things we surround ourselves with. Thus, architectural photography becomes the art of the indirect; its task is to represent something that cannot be represented. For Böhme, as I mentioned in the introduction to this chapter, architecture is essentially about creating atmospheres, and atmospheres cannot be photographed as such but possibly evoked or at least pointed to, through indirect means and unconventional images. In the

---

28   Norberg-Schulz 1980, p. 5.
29   Otero-Pailos 2007, pp. 220–241.
30   Griffero 2010, p. 81, mentions Norberg-Schulz speaking in passing of *genius loci* but suggests that his understanding of this is altogether too banal and generalising.
31   Böhme 2019a, pp. 116, 119. Cf. pp. 112–133.

background of Böhme's position on architectural photography we find the reference to the living body's relationship to existential space, a relationship that is corporeal and synesthetic and therefore, first and foremost, an atmospheric relationship to a space that cannot be reduced to geometry.[32]

To be physically present in a room means not only to be positioned in a room according to certain geometric coordinates but also to be in a room that is permeated by a certain atmosphere. The atmosphere is conveyed through the bodily sensation of being present in the room. The problem with much of the twentieth century's oculocentric architecture, at least according to Böhme, was that "rationality, construction technology, [and] functionality" determined the construction and not our human existence in the atmospheric space.[33] A human being as a physical body and not a living and experiencing body has taken centre stage.[34] However, the remedy for this atmospheric oblivion is not to turn only to the experience of space, as if geometric space were irrelevant. Rather, by recalling the importance of atmospheric space, the remedy is to try to understand how they are connected. Without the walls, ceilings, floors, furniture and other things that answer the question "what?" in relation to space it becomes impossible to answer the question "how?", which concerns the way we experience the space in which we are physically present. The experience of atmospheres in a building is therefore dependent on interactions with the things that make up the building. To experience a building or a room means to experience oneself in the room and also to experience the room around oneself.

Similar to the architects above, the atmospheric phenomenologists therefore emphasise the importance of materials for the atmosphere. A material radiates a certain atmosphere that corresponds with a certain way of life. When describing something as vague as atmosphere, this is often done by pointing out something as concrete as a material and a colour to describe the difference between, for example, the atmosphere in Gothenburg's versus Stockholm's inner city: yellow Dutch brick versus ochre-coloured plaster facades. Note: even if I do not physically touch these surfaces, the impression is tactile and not just visual. By knowing and feeling the tools at their disposal, the architect can produce a certain atmosphere: geometry, shape and proportion, but also light, colour and tone.[35] When Böhme describes the atmosphere in a church hall – and he means one of the great European cathedrals – in a certain city or on the stage

---

32    Cf. Böhme 2013, p. 105.
33    Böhme 2013, p. 115.
34    Böhme 2013, p. 121. Cf. pp. 122–126.
35    Böhme 2013, p. 18. Cf. p. 162.

of a theatre, he describes in more or less detail how such a room is planned, built and furnished. If it is the construction and staging of the room itself, then a change in the room, such as a lower ceiling, a cooler temperature of the lighting, replacing pews with plastic chairs or the impossibility of opening windows, also means a change in the atmosphere.

As far as architecture is concerned, atmospheric phenomenologists would not say that a certain material necessarily leads to a certain atmosphere, for example, that natural wood produces a warm feeling in a room. Even apart from cultural differences in the meanings of materials, the realisation of the experience of space as synesthetic means that it is the various materials, forms and shapes in harmony with each other that produce the atmosphere. The skill of the skilful architect consists precisely in the ability to use a combination of the material means at their disposal to actually produce the atmosphere that they also seek to stage. Such knowledge is a kind of experiential or practical knowledge, which arises in the concrete work rather than through a learnt recipe that is then also applied.[36] It is precisely through a thorough knowledge of materials, building processes, planning and other factors that the architect possesses their atmospheric competence.

A prerequisite for the production of all atmospheres, regardless of the architect's skill and ability to create a certain atmosphere, is that the people who experience the atmosphere in a church, for example, are in some sense also always co-producers of this atmosphere. Surroundings and history also play a role. Not infrequently, for example, the presence of an old town centre or the knowledge of a historical event surrounding a particular building can contribute to the atmosphere. In the former case I think of Sigtuna, one of the first Swedish towns, with a centre that is characterised by historical charm, and in the latter, a visit to Berggasse 19 in central Vienna is given meaning from the fact that this was Sigmund Freud's home and workplace for many years. Both contribute to the atmosphere of the city or building in a way that is beyond the control of the city planner or architect. Both of these places are personal examples, as it is possible to be indifferent to both the charm of Sigtuna and the significance of Freud, but the point holds even if the examples are changed: there are atmospheric circumstances in the production of a building that the architect can relate to but hardly control.

There are risks in talking about architecture as atmosphere. One of these, as noted by several phenomenologists, is that an interest in the atmospheres of buildings easily lends itself to and "aesthetic economy" that understands

---

36    On practical knowledge, see Bornemark and Svenaeus 2009.

the whole of human life in terms of staging and where architecture also becomes part of the (over)production of aesthetic needs.[37] However, the realisation that all buildings also have an atmosphere needs not result in an uncritical approach to such atmospheres. In the first place, phenomenology is about recognising the experience of atmospheres as such, in order to be able to take a critical approach to it. Secondly, the architect must be aware of the risk of merely constructing backdrops for people's aesthetic lifestyle projects.[38] Architecture must become an architecture for people, not people in an abstract sense but for the people who inhabit the spaces. Which design language this results in concretely is not a question that phenomenology can answer from its own competence if it is to remain phenomenology. However, it is worth pointing out that neither the phenomenologists nor the atmospherically interested architects above are concerned with any kind of nostalgic, neo-romantic or neo-classical architecture. Rather, the point is to remind us that atmospheres are an important aspect of architectural work that has been lost in an architecture that has become too eye-centred, facade-oriented and technical. Based on the realisation that not all atmospheres are inherently complete and finished, Griffero believes that the task of the architect can be to create places that invite certain possibilities, abilities and sensations and that can realise a good atmosphere. He cites the example of the hospital and asks for the architectural conditions that create a less tense atmosphere for the visitor.[39] In the nineteenth century, British art critic and writer John Ruskin spoke not only of "fidelity to the material" but also of imperfection as a virtue for an architecture that wants to be expressive and alive.[40] Perhaps it is precisely the realisation of the sensory quality of materiality, as well as imperfection as a principle, that can be said to be phenomenology's contribution to an architecture of atmospheres. In other words, it calls for an architecture that allows the visitor to co-create the atmosphere.


*Production of Atmospheres*

We have seen that, at least among some architects, an understanding of architecture as a way of producing atmospheres is combined with a critique of an architecture that is exclusively for the eye, to the detriment

---

37    Böhme 2016; Böhme 2013, p. 8.
38    Böhme 2013, pp. 175–176.
39    Griffero 2014, p. 37.
40    Ruskin 2009, pp. 48–49.

of a more multimodal understanding of architecture. Architecture therefore emerges as a clear and central example of the aesthetic work described by phenomenology, which consists of producing atmospheres. Among architects, practical knowledge is, so to speak, in the hands and acquired through experience. Although the theoretical knowledge of atmospheres has fallen behind in our time, this does not mean that this other form of knowledge is missing. And while the practical knowledge of atmospheric production among architects may be difficult to articulate in words in a reasonably satisfactory way, the realisation of practical atmospheric production helps to deepen the theoretical understanding of atmospheres, especially in terms of how production should be understood. However, the question of the actual relationship between the reception and production of atmospheres remains. Are they contrasts or can they be thought of as, at least in some cases, interdependent?

Is it possible, even for those with the necessary practical knowledge, to stage what kind of atmosphere a particular building should exude? I mentioned in the previous chapter the open-plan office as an example of an interior design of a space whose original purpose was to promote an atmosphere of spontaneous and mutual exchange of ideas but which has instead come to increase stress in workplaces and encroach on the need for privacy.[41] This example seemingly suggests that it can be almost impossible to know in advance what kind of atmosphere will actually result from a building or design process. There is certainly an element of unpredictability in aesthetic work because it involves knowledge in the form of judgement rather than causation. However, Griffero, from whom the office landscape example is taken, argues that the difficulties of staging atmospheres in architecture should not be exaggerated to the point of seeming impossible.[42] Often architects succeed perfectly well. However, like any human activity where there may be several competing objectives, the risk of failure can never be completely avoided. Moreover, as mentioned above, atmospheres are never fully finished. They also depend on how they are received. In addition, there are other factors that influence the outcome: less skilful architects, of course, but also limited financial resources, the system of the construction industry and the ambiguity of the contract. Nevertheless, the production of atmospheres is a genuine skill. The aesthetic work of the architect in the process of producing an atmosphere is, if we follow the architects above, a compositional work in which the architect, based

---

41    Griffero 2010, pp. 153–154.
42    Griffero 2014, pp. 35–36.

on their knowledge of materials, building processes, planning and so on, brings together materials, forms and volumes in a way that creates a unique resonance. In other words, it is working *with* materials that already exist in the world (even if they are artificial composites) and arranging them in relation to each other, rather than a creation out of nothing. Thus, production here does not mean creating atmospheres that previously did not exist at all but, rather, producing in the more original sense of the word, namely bringing them forth and making them present.[43] This does not mean that the architect's role as an active producer disappears, but we have to imagine the architect as someone who is themself receptive to the potential atmospheres that the composition of materials, forms and volumes can produce. The art of architecture as understood in this case is experiential knowledge acquired through education but also – and perhaps primarily? – through personal experiences of atmospheres. In the earlier typological contrast between the craftsman and the engineer, the architect is more reminiscent of the craftsman in that the relationship to the world must transcend the purely instrumental.

This also puts the relationship between the production and reception of atmospheres in a new light: they do not merely coincide but are intimately connected and cannot be easily separated. The producing architect is also a human being surrounded by atmospheres who acquires his or her competence from the practical experience of them. The fact that it is possible to produce atmospheres, and thus in some sense to be active in relation to them, presupposes and fulfils the mediopassivity of the human being that I mentioned in previous chapters. Thus, unless production is contrasted with reception, the possibility of producing atmospheres does not mean that their spontaneous character must be illusory or less genuine. Nevertheless, as we are surrounded by atmospheres, we are relatively active in our reception of them, like the tennis player returning a serve. As our experience of the possibilities we have in receiving them grows, so do our ways of relating to them in terms of critique, but also as production.[44] But just as we do not seem to be able to completely free ourselves from atmospheres in our criticism of them, neither do we seem to be able to produce them completely at will. The production of atmospheres presupposes a knowledge based on our own reflective experience of atmospheres, not only as their producers but primarily as those who are themselves surrounded by atmospheres.

---

43    Gumbrecht 2004, pp. xiii–xiv.
44    Certeau 1984, pp. 34–39.

5.

LIVING IN ATMOSPHERES

In the first chapter, when I introduced atmosphere as a phenomenon, I moved from the gas enveloping the earth, across the Sahara Desert and the fog-shrouded streetlights of New York to a house on Mühlweg in Friedberg. In other words, I started from the atmosphere as a boundary between earth and space and then travelled with the help of literature across nature to the city and home. To find out what it means in practice to live in atmospheres, I will now repeat this journey in the opposite direction. By examining how we live in atmospheres, we become even more aware of how they work and, at the same time, learn something about how we ourselves live in the home, the city or nature.

## The Home

When Andreas Maier's young alter ego in *Die Straße* visits a neighbouring house that looks much the same as his own home, he is filled with an uncanny feeling. Small details such as the colour of the facade, the size of the windows, the smell of the house and the accumulation of objects at the foot of the staircase are enough for him to perceive the "atmosphere of the foreign dwelling" as a separate, distinct world from his own.[1] This is a classic example of the expression of the uncanny: something alien asserting itself through something familiar. It also teaches us something about atmospheres in the home.

Although not as uncomfortable as the young Maier, there is always something special about entering someone else's home. Should I take off my shoes or not? In Sweden and Japan, yes; in England and France, no. But how does this particular household in which I am a guest want me to behave? Where can I sit? What books are on the bookshelves? What are the scents that greet me? What is the view from the windows? Is there

---

1    Maier 2015, pp. 9, 7.

a friendly atmosphere among those who live there? Even if there is an unmistakable atmosphere in the unfamiliar home that greets me at the door, it is not always obvious enough that I can read it. As a guest, I might first ask myself whether it is inviting, cosy, opulent, strict or mainly functional.

While there may be a basic tone to the atmosphere in a home, there are also different modulations of this depending on time and place. The atmospheres in the morning, at noon, in the evening and at night are different. Different rooms also hold differences: as a guest, there is a significant difference between visiting someone's living room or kitchen, compared to being in someone's bathroom, bedroom or basement. The former are at least semi-public: they are where we are welcomed as guests and where we also find the side of the home that the residents want to show off. The other rooms are more or less private, even for invited guests. There is a good reason why in psychoanalysis the cellar is associated with the drives, the unconscious and the repressed. Gaston Bachelard rightly speaks of the cellar as "the *dark entity* of the house".[2] If I go to the basement the first time I am invited into someone's home, I will be met with an atmosphere that is markedly different from that of the kitchen, for example. If the owner were to realise that I had immediately descended into the basement, I would probably have to explain what I was doing there. There are many ways to talk about what a home is, but one way to talk about home is as an organ of atmosphere management.[3] Just as there may be a need to regulate the temperature in the home, there may also be a need to regulate the atmosphere or atmospheres.

But what is a home? Even if we ignore the fact that the home has a history and limit ourselves to what constitutes a home for people in the Western world today, the question is not simple. There are a variety of living arrangements (collective, nuclear family, single household) and buildings (house, apartment, room in a dormitory) that are people's homes, but also many who are homeless in one way or another. Philosophical reflection on the home does not provide a clear answer to the question, either: Emanuele Coccia argues that philosophy has never really been interested in the home, despite the fact that we spend so much time there, preferring instead to talk about the city.[4] But, in fact, we don't live in cities but in homes, he points out; sooner or later we all have to go home. And home can be a hotel or an apartment, a sofa or a skyscraper. The form varies, but the home must have

---

2    Bachelard 1994, p. 18; cf. Funke 2014, pp. 101–102.
3    Cf. Schmitz 2019a, p. 213.
4    Coccia 2021, pp. 5–7.

some definite form to be a home. However, Griffero warns against nostalgic as well as utopian and pragmatic tendencies in philosophical reflections on the home, which in fact presuppose that such reflections already exists.[5] Even outside the circle of phenomenologists interested in atmosphere, we have already encountered a number of philosophers who have analysed home and dwelling in depth, such as Heidegger, Bollnow and Bachelard, making Coccia's claim seem somewhat exaggerated.[6]

At the same time, it is not impossible that Coccia has a point, both historically and in relation to our time. The home, as the sphere of reproduction and, until the industrial revolution, also the sphere of production, has often been unfavourably contrasted with the city as the sphere of politics and thought. If the home has traditionally been the woman's sphere, the city has been the man's. A series of such contrasts has probably haunted the distinction between home and city, but, as Coccia points out, this is all the more reason to pay attention to the home in order to critically visualise the injustices and inequalities that might otherwise be reproduced into the future. To this we can add the fact that the home is also the place where we usually spend the six to eight hours a day sleeping. During sleep we are at the mercy of other people; we are unconscious and remain unproductive and inaccessible to any modernisation efforts.[7] The bedroom and the bed are the parts of the home where we physically as well as symbolically adopt a completely different relationship to space and to the world than the upright concentration of wakefulness: we lie down horizontally, and almost everything is out of reach even when we stretch out our arms. To dwell is to have somewhere to retreat to sleep, but to sleep is to regress for a while. Are the bedroom and also sleep reasons for the relative invisibility of the home, attempts to forget aspects of our humanity that do not fit the image of a human being as active, independent and conscious? We can at least conclude from this that the very definition of a home becomes a position that raises several critical questions about history and the present.

To get straight to the question of what a home is, we should first of all avoid identifying a home with a particular kind of building. Apart from the fact that even nomads must be said to have a home, the identification risks turning the home, at least in the imagination, into a static construction. Having a home is not only a state but also very much a dynamic process:

---

5     Griffero 2020, p. 115.

6     In addition to Bachelard 1994, see Heidegger 2000, pp. 145–164; Bollnow 2011, pp. 121–179.

7     Crary 2013; Bollnow 2011, pp. 155–179; Funke 2014, pp. 105–109.

dwelling and being on the move are both part of the basic existential conditions of human beings.[8] In the previous chapter we encountered the Danish word *hjemliggørelse*, which has no equivalent in Swedish but could be translated into English as to inhabit something. Here, we retain the association with the word habitat or home. Inhabiting something denotes the act of appropriating a specific space so that it becomes our own in the sense of feeling at home there.[9] To inhabit also has a counterpart in a Greek word from Stoic philosophy, *oikeiosis*, which also refers to the active transformation of a space into a home, at least as it is used in contemporary philosophy.[10] In Stoic ethics, the term mainly refers to the gradual growth of the young person into public morality and could be translated as appropriation. But the term literally describes the process of making something one's *oikos* – a Greek word for home or house –, and thus it can also be understood as making something one's home, housing or habitation. This is a double process of appropriation: not only turning the dwelling we have just moved into to a home but also establishing ourselves in this home by adapting to it. The act of inhabiting a space – *hjemliggørelse* or *oikeiosis* – is a mediopassive act. To inhabit a space and thus to make it one's own, in other words, a home, is not only about experiencing the space as an object of our sight, touch or hearing, but first and foremost about living the space. "Inhabited space transcends geometric space", as Bachelard writes.[11]

The act or event that most clearly exemplifies the process of making a space one's own home is moving. Moving into a new home is a concrete form of inhabiting, and, similarly, moving from a previous home can be described as de-habiting.[12] Moving – at least in the deeper sense of the word – is not simply a matter of the people who make up the household changing residence. To begin with, it is a sophisticated logistical exercise, where furniture and objects have to be packed, transported, unpacked and put in their proper places in the new home. But above all, it is a whole context of life that must change residence. Our homes are made up of relationships, not only with other people, although they are of course central, but also

---

8    Guzzoni 2017, pp. 11–12.
9    Gammelgaard Nielsen 2021, pp. 118–119.
10   See Coccia 2021, pp. 17–18; Fuchs, 2018, p. 311, including note 4.
11   Bachelard 1994, p. 147.
12   On the phenomenology of moving, see Hasse 2020. Hasse points out on pp. 10–12 that there is a fundamental difference between "moving" and "fleeing", and my discussion here only concerns the former. On memories as embodied by buildings as such, see Assmann 2007; Connerton 1989.

with the things we surround ourselves with, including plants and animals: potted plants, gardens, allotments, our pets if we have them and, further, the more or less domesticated birds, deer, cats and foxes that surround the house. The objects of the home are not just things but things with which we have a history, which we use in our daily lives, which constitute our homes to the extent that our domesticity can only be separated from them with difficulty. They cannot be reduced to a use value, narrowly understood as pragmatic utility, but have acquired an aura through our interaction with them (and their interaction with us). The home carries memories that are embodied in our furniture, objects and rooms. These are sedimented traces of our lives. Memories are also revived and brought into new light by the move, as objects lose some of the obviousness that they held when they occupied a certain place in the former home. The transport of things in the move is thus not primarily a logistical problem but an existential limit situation. The move is a caesura, an interruption where everything changes: our relationship to the home, to the things we surround ourselves with, to the neighbours and the neighbourhood, to our household and to ourselves. The relationship with the home that belonged to us, and to which we ourselves belonged just as much, ceases with the move, and a different relationship with a new home must be established. To illustrate the radical nature of the move, it can be likened to shedding one's skin: the home as a kind of third skin, alongside the biological skin and clothing, is replaced by another skin.[13] In and through all this, the move is also a change of atmosphere.

The process of changing the atmosphere takes longer than the actual moving of things. Packing up your belongings for the move evokes memories, and with memories the atmospheres that dominate the home also become clearer. At the same time, the atmospheres gradually disintegrate as things disappear into moving boxes and furniture is carried out. The move itself is characterised by an interim atmosphere of no-longer-inhabiting and not-yet-inhabiting. There is no longer a real "home" but only a state of transit between two "aways". The atmosphere that lingers in the increasingly empty rooms becomes a kind of residual atmosphere, characterised above all by the fact that the things that filled the room have now been removed. From being affectively charged, the rooms gradually revert to a more neutral, geometric state, although reminiscences of what once took place in them may linger, even after the previous occupants have left. In preparing to move, we prepare for an affective departure (which can be a relief as well as a grief) from a familiar environment. But atmospheres,

---

13    Hasse 2020, pp. 88–90; see also Sigurdson 2022.

like things, cannot be packed up and transported to the new home. Moving into a new dwelling, turning it into a home in a process of *oikeiosis,* must therefore be a form of staging, aesthetic work in the sense that we have familiarised ourselves with in the previous chapter. The purpose of aesthetic work after the move is not primarily to create a beautiful home in the trivial sense but to produce atmospheres that make us feel at home.

Moving into a new home is not just about unpacking. The things in their boxes appear to be disorganised, and the rooms, unfamiliar. Initially, it is about creating an order in the rooms where things can be found at all. Gradually, moving in turns into arranging the unpacked items and furniture in such a way that the house goes from being just a space with walls, floors, ceilings and doors to a dwelling, populated not only by ourselves but also by the things that make us feel at home. The house without all our objects has been likened by Ceccio to a desert and "a purely mineral structure".[14] The purpose of the furnishings is to create an atmosphere that transcends the atmosphere of a warehouse. Things and furniture that no longer fit in are relegated to the basement or attic – "the graveyards of the house's things" – or are thrown away or donated.[15] The aim is for the new home to also achieve what Schmitz calls "a holistic 'climate' for life".[16] We experience this holistic climate for life not with individual senses in an intentional act of sensing but with our entire body. What constitutes such an atmospheric climate is, of course, dependent on personal preferences in dialectical interaction with cultural and social beliefs. What is constant is rather the very process of establishing an atmosphere of well-being that makes us feel at home and not just on a temporary visit. We must relearn how to dwell.

But what is an atmosphere of well-being? In short, it is an atmosphere that supports, in a timely and affective way, the various uses of the home that we may need: to be alone, to socialise, to celebrate, to sleep, to wash, to clean, to cook and eat, to play, to pray, to read, to make love, to drink wine, to make music, to dream and so on. Achieving such an atmosphere of well-being does not happen by itself or very quickly. It depends first of all on the gradual development of proxemic spatial competence, the ability to move intuitively around the room without bumping into the furniture, but it is also, and above all, about settling in oneself affectively. In a sense, creating an atmosphere of well-being, of homeliness, is an ongoing process, even

---

14    Ceccio 2021, p. 43.
15    Ceccio 2021, p. 50.
16    Schmitz 2019a, p. 220.

when the move is complete. We are constantly furnishing and rearranging our rooms, big and small, not necessarily in search of perfection but, rather, in search of variety. An atmosphere of well-being is a living atmosphere, not one where everything is familiar or everything is foreign but one that strikes a balance between these poles. The creation of such an atmosphere is not a process that is first planned and then executed; it is a process that gradually emerges in an interaction with things and space.[17] "Settling in" is an experience of a growing and spontaneous resonance between things, space and ourselves, rather than something we can fully control.

Appropriating a specific space as one's home is not, as one might think, only about producing atmospheres but also, and equally, about drawing a boundary with the atmospheres that surround us and threaten to overwhelm us. According to Schmitz, it is the act of "enclosure" that defines housing.[18] This enclosing act has a double function: on the one hand, it protects us from external atmospheres in their raw state, but on the other hand, it also serves as a way of relating to them. In the exterior, in its unboundedness we encounter a kind of atmospheric uncanniness, which in the past might have been about the forest, the night or the sky, but today is equally about the concrete jungle and, for the sensitive Maier in *Die Straße,* the strange and alien atmosphere of the neighbouring houses. This atmospherically raw state is existentially impossible to stay in for any length of time, and the creation of a home is therefore an act of demarcating a space by enclosing it, thus managing the atmospheres in a way that makes them possible to live in and with. The home is a place that, in Griffero's words, "allows us to capture, cultivate and administer external atmospheres otherwise out of control".[19] But the border between inside and outside always remains ambivalent, as it implies both protection and vulnerability. Establishing a boundary – geometric as well as affective – that surrounds a concrete space in the infinity of spatiality through enclosure is probably as humanly necessary as the skin that separates my body from other bodies.

Enclosure is a form of the humanisation of space; it is turning space into a place. Having a home can be understood as having your own place to retreat to, a place that is not open to everyone.[20] By delimiting the space of the home from other spaces that do not belong to the home, it also establishes the spatial condition of possibility for psychologically

---

17   Hasse 2020, p. 145.
18   Schmitz 2019a, pp. 238–257.
19   Griffero 2020, p. 119.
20   Bollnow 2011, pp. 124–125.

developing a separate, delimited identity, a self.[21] In *A Room of One's Own,* Virginia Woolf links the quest for a separate creative and independent voice for women with the need for a room of one's own in the literal sense, where creative work can be carried out undisturbed. If the physical space is not demarcated, the affective space cannot be demarcated either. But just as the skin both separates me from the outside world and connects me to it by responding to its stimuli, the boundary of the home will not only be a boundary *from* the outside world and the infinite expanse of space but also a boundary *to* the outside world.

In the home, this affective and concrete material boundary between inside and outside is always regulated in several ways. Doors, windows, chimneys, sliding walls and garages are all thresholds where the boundary between inside and outside no longer remains absolute but appears as a membrane that is porous to varying degrees. The home is and must always be a dynamic play between the foreign and the familiar. If the walls enclosing the home close too tightly, the atmosphere becomes oppressive and claustrophobic. As a symbol of this, Björn Runge's 2003 film *Daybreak* depicts how a layer of bricks is commissioned to seal the windows and doors of an elderly couple who want to protect themselves from what they perceive as an increasingly dangerous outside world. If, on the other hand, the home consisted only of a roof over one's head, it would hardly be a home at all since the boundary between inside and outside almost disappears. The home seems to be no more hermetically sealed than it is boundlessly open. That there are homes that can be experienced as prisons in their rigid closedness (the neurotic home) is thus no more surprising than that there are homes that never manage to establish any form of intimacy in their unwillingness to draw boundaries (the psychotic home). Of course, these are not diagnoses of the people in these houses but, rather, attempts to capture atmospheric experiences.

Thus, there must always be openings in the porous membrane that constitutes the outer boundaries of the home in order for it to be a home. These openings, concrete ones in the form of doors, windows and so on, constitute the thresholds of the home in the sense of a passage where a transition takes place between one atmosphere and another. Architecture can be said to be a form of atmospheric management that in the house represents the boundary or threshold between inside and outside; we can think of Frank Lloyd Wright's 1939 house *Falllingwater* as a commentary

---

21   Funke 2014, pp. 111–134.

on this.[22] Moving into a new home with all that this entails is a unique way of crossing such a threshold. "A *Schwelle* 'threshold' is a zone", writes Benjamin. "Transformation, passage, wave action are in the word *schwellen*, swell, and etymology ought not to overlook these senses."[23] But thresholds remain thresholds even in everyday life. Although these thresholds are culture-dependent – does the porch of a traditional American house belong to the home or to the street outside? – the house is not a home if there is no regulation between inside and outside in the form of a threshold. The nature of the threshold is that it is ambivalent. To be on the threshold of a home is thus to be in an ambivalent state *between* inside and outside. Therefore, the instruments that regulate these thresholds also become significant: the window that protects against the wind also opens to ventilate; the door that shuts out the outside world also opens to welcome the guest. Separating the home and the world and linking them together become two sides of the same coin. As Georg Simmel has pointed out, the door has a deeply human meaning: here we limit ourselves while retaining the freedom to transcend this limitation.[24] The window is mainly dedicated to the eye, and its primary function is to let us look out, while the open door allows our whole body to pass through, both on the way in and on the way out. Through such thresholds, the outside world seeps into the home, and the home reaches out to the world.

However, the concrete, physical thresholds of the dwelling that is a home are not its only thresholds. The twentieth-century media revolution, with telephone, radio, television and eventually all the technologies that emerged around digital communication, has meant that the outside world has moved into the home. Some would argue that the outside world has colonised the home. But if these are the more tangible porous membranes that make the home's separation from the outside world ambivalent, we should not forget other membranes in the form of the modern home's infrastructure: electricity, sewage, water and the constant inflow and outflow of mail, consumer goods, food, waste and rubbish. Although the home is and must be enclosed in Schmitz's sense of being a home, this does not contradict the fact that it must also be very much an organism living in symbiosis with the outside world in order to function. If the water and electricity are cut off, if the rubbish is not collected, this affects the home almost immediately, as it is not only a life-support machine for its

---

22   Harrison 1992, pp. 232–238.
23   Benjamin 1999, p. 494. On thresholds and threshold experiences, see Sigurdson 2024.
24   Simmel 2001, pp. 55–61.

occupants but also its atmosphere. The atmosphere of the home is always established in some sort of interaction with the atmosphere of what is not a home, and when this exchange changes or ceases, the atmosphere of the home is also affected.

If inhabiting from this perspective consists of managing atmospheres by regulating the relationship between inside and outside in a way that promotes well-being, then this is also a way of saying that the home must strike a balance between the familiar and the unfamiliar. In *The Poetics of Space,* Bachelard reiterates that the home must offer spaces that are secretive and intimate, not accessible to everyone – wardrobes, dressers, drawers, corners – without which we could not dream.[25] Similarly, he argues that the secrecy and intimacy that is materially manifested in the verticality of basements and attics risks being lost in the purely horizontal home.[26] The home without basement and attic contributes to shaping a one-dimensional human being, and Bachelard consequently laments that there are no real homes in Paris or other big cities, only "superimposed boxes" in the form of skyscrapers without basements.[27] Our homes shape who we are because their spatiality shapes the way we inhabit them.

Beyond the cultural and class specificity of the ideal of a house with a basement and attic, Bachelard touches on the realisation that the specific form of spatiality of the home is characterised by always transcending the purely functional and geometric. The home, whatever its concrete, material form, is an atmospheric space if it is a home. For Maier's young alter ego in *Die Straße,* the experience of the unfamiliar in the midst of the familiar became so dominant that the atmosphere in the neighbouring house was perceived as uncanny. Here he is confronted with the traces of other people's lives. If he had grown up in this strange house with its different smells, its different lighting and different rooms, he would have been different, he says.[28] But how would young Maier have reacted if everything in the neighbouring house had been the same as in his own home: the same smells, the same lighting and the same objects at the foot of the stairs? Wouldn't the sheer repetition give rise to a corresponding anxiety, as if from something all too familiar that should have been different?

---

25    Bachelard 1994, pp. 78–79, 81, 88–89, 136, *et passim.*
26    Bachelard 1994, pp. 17, 26–27.
27    Bachelard 1994, p. 26.
28    Maier 2015, p. 10.

If Bachelard is right that "the house is our corner of the world", Maier's novel reminds us of the precariousness of the balance that maintains that corner.[29]

Not only do I shape the atmosphere of a home, but the atmosphere of the home also affects who I am. If the home changes, I change, and vice versa. The atmosphere of a home, not only other people's but also one's own, can be oppressive and uncanny, and the move can be liberating. But without a home, a home that possesses some form of permanence and stability and that harbours an atmosphere of well-being, we cannot survive existentially in the long run. The purely nomadic existence, at least in its late capitalist form, seems as rare and existentially unsustainable as the attitude of the man and woman in Runge's film who wall themselves into their house to protect themselves from the surrounding city and its threatening atmosphere. But if the city is not always threatening, what is its atmosphere?

## The City

Around the lit streetlamps in Louise Glück's poem "Cornwall" the fog swirls; things that were previously clear become increasingly blurred in the night. This interplay of light, darkness and fog is a recognisable mood of an urban landscape. I am thinking, for example, of the American photographer Alfred Stieglitz (1864–1946), who in his images of New York wanted to capture the life of the city precisely through his deliberately chosen (relative) optical blurring, his fondness for fog and sometimes even a chiaroscuro in the play between light and darkness. For Stieglitz, urban photography was not about a visual representation of buildings but about trying to reproduce the atmosphere of New York. In a 1915 photograph, "From the Back Window", he captures a contrast between darkness and light as well as between the more modest houses in the foreground, where laundry hangs outside on a line, and the modern skyscrapers in the background with their uniform lighting. The high humidity in New York means that fog is a recurring phenomenon that characterises the city's atmosphere, almost as much as the artificial lighting and the many skyscrapers. In countless films, we encounter the Manhattan skyline at night in panoramic city views that tend to linger on its silhouette. Here, the image of the city that never sleeps is imprinted on our cultural imagination in a visual but also emotional way. Although the image of a city in fog

---

29   Bachelard 1994, p. 4.

is just that, an image, poetic, photographic or cinematic, it has what we might call a synesthetic appeal. Walking through a foggy landscape is an immersive experience that not only affects the visual sense. When Glück chooses such an image, she certainly does so because she knows that it evokes certain affects in the reader.

Lit streetlamps in fog provide a typical atmosphere associated with the city, one of many. And it is typical not only of New York but of countless other cities. What is typical of the more general urban atmosphere? How can we talk about urban atmospheres in a way that does not get lost in the anecdotal but manages to express some general features of living in the city atmosphere? First, we must begin with what a city is. If the ancient city was characterised by a temple in the centre of the city and a wall that surrounded and separated it from everything that was not a city, this hardly characterises the modern metropolis, where the centre is usually its financial district and the geographical boundary seems to be extendable outwards without a clear end. Often the modern city has not one but several centres and has incorporated what are called suburbs within its own administrative boundaries. Unlike the ancient, medieval and early modern city, the modern metropolis is virtually impossible to plan or survey, both in terms of population and territory, even though, ironically, planning and surveying are among the features that are central to the values of the modern city. Adding to this lack of overview are the secret cities that surround the modern city as its peripheral endpoints: the self-imposed secret cities (for example, gated communities) and the secret cities that are hidden away (for example, shanty towns).[30] Approaching the city as an object of critical reflection also offers a number of different perspectives. We can talk about the city in terms of its buildings and planning; its various functions; its economic, political and social organisation; its infrastructure; its geographical position and environment, and so on. All these possible perspectives are certainly relevant for talking about atmospheres in the city, but, as has been pointed out by the atmospherologists, the city and its relationship to the emotions have often been overshadowed in this diversity of academic perspectives.[31]

Is there an atmosphere in New York, Paris or any other similar big city that is specific to that city? The tourism industry, hand in hand with the film industry, easily lead us to assume that there should be a characteristic atmosphere of all large cities. Indeed, for metropolises like these, it is not

---

30    Dahlberg 2010, pp. 5–7.
31    Hasse 2015b, p. 43.

only advertising and film that create our images of them but also their history, as well as how they are referred to in literature and popular culture in general. To take a not very contemporary example, Goethe (1749–1832) had grown up with etchings of the ruins of Rome by "some of the skillful predecessors of Piranesi", with which his father had decorated one of the attics of the house.[32] These made a great impression on the young Goethe. When he finally embarked on his Italian journey at the age of 37, he did so to experience in person what he knew from the reproductions art: to visit the buildings of Renaissance architect Andrea Palladio but also to finally see for himself the Rome he had come to know over many years through the etchings. In fact, he was disappointed. Although he eventually became more content, Rome was not at all what he had imagined; it was noisy and messy. The atmosphere conveyed by the etchings at home turned out to be nothing like the real Rome he encountered when he entered the Porta del Popolo. Everything was familiar yet so alien. Goethe left for Naples and Sicily but eventually returned, before reluctantly going back to Weimar. Even when Goethe published his account of his Italian journey more than forty years later, the image of Rome he conveys is reminiscent of Giovanni Battista Piranesi's (1720–1778) etchings in the *Vedute di Roma*, where we encounter an aged, romanticised image of the city. Piranesi's etchings became particularly important to Goethe once he returned home and may well have influenced parts of his account. We can recognise Goethe's experience that the reality of the city does not correspond to our perception of it, and a key aspect of this is the city's atmosphere, which is one of the things we expect to experience when we visit a new city. But perhaps there is no specific atmosphere to the city? Is it simply a marketing ploy to bring tourists or businesses?

In a discussion on medieval cities, American sociologist Lewis Mumford names some examples of such cities by attributing different colours to them: red Sienna, black and white Genoa, grey Paris, variegated Florence and golden Venice.[33] The colours are not to be understood here as mere visual impressions but as a synesthetic: an attempt to summarise the character of the cities, where golden Venice, above other contemporary cities, embodies an urban structure that, in the fourteenth to sixteenth centuries, managed to combine continuity with change and uniformity with variety in its organisation of quarters and districts. Through its dynamic and organic structure, Renaissance Venice managed to transcend its walls, figuratively

---

32   Goethe 1970, p. 16; Goethe 2013, pp. 133–134, 164. Cf. Tschudi 2015.
33   Mumford 1989, pp. 321–328.

speaking, and, thanks to its islands, to divide the city into different zones, which not only reduced the pressure on St Mark's Square but also gave its six quarters or districts their own function and relative autonomy. The canals acted as natural boundaries between the neighbourhoods but also as their connecting links. The result was an aesthetically pleasing whole which, according to Mumford, attracted more artists to depict it than any other city since the fifteenth century.

Not all cities are Venice, but Mumford's description of Venice as a functional and aesthetically pleasing dynamic whole illustrates something of how urban atmospheres should be understood. According to Jürgen Hasse, one of the phenomenologists most concerned with urban atmospheres, it is the neighbourhood that can be characterised by a specific atmosphere, not the city as such.[34] When Hasse speaks of "quarters" (in German *Quartier*), what he means is what in English is called a neighbourhood, albeit in an informal rather than publicly defined sense. Gärdet in Stockholm, Majorna in Gothenburg and Möllevången in Malmö are all neighbourhoods in this sense, associated with a certain atmosphere that we may be familiar with without being able to express it fully. The district is manageable in size, which means that the atmosphere can be concretely localised. The city as a whole is too large, too diffuse, to be characterised by a single atmosphere. However, this does not mean that the atmosphere of the district is an atmosphere as static as its buildings; the atmosphere is something created in and through the dynamic flows that cross the district in interaction with its material physiognomy. The atmospheres have a performative dynamic; they are something that happens rather than something that is.

If we take Mumford's description of Renaissance Venice as an illustration, it is the individual neighbourhoods, each dedicated to one of Venice's six guilds, that carry particular atmospheres, atmospheres that were shaped by the activities of the particular guilds that were located in the particular neighbourhoods. This does not mean that Venice as a city is devoid of atmosphere, but its atmosphere as a city exists more in the interpenetration and superimposition of the different atmospheres of the neighbourhoods than in a uniform and easily distinguishable atmosphere.[35] What we as tourists expect is perhaps a more homogeneous atmosphere, which we project onto the whole of Venice as a city (of which we may not see much). If we were to settle there, preferably during the Renaissance, a more nuanced experience of the different atmospheres of its neighbourhoods and

---

34   Hasse 2015b, pp. 205–206; Hasse 2015a, p. 85.
35   Hasse 2015b, p. 185.

districts would probably eventually emerge. In contemporary cities, which are both far more complex and far more heterogeneous than Renaissance Venice, it is even more clear that the unique atmosphere of the city must be an agglomeration of atmospheres rather than a single atmosphere. Perhaps it is this very agglomeration of atmospheres that constitutes the specifically urban atmosphere?

What characterises the contemporary city, especially the metropolis, is what Hasse, inspired by Schmitz but also Simmel, calls its "chaotic diversity", where we cannot separate the components from each other but experience them as a confusing whole.[36] In his 1903 essay "The Metropolis and Mental Life", Simmel argues that the person living in the city is subjected to such a "intensification of emotional life", due to its "swift and continuous shift of external and internal stimuli", that they are forced to distance themself from emotional involvement in the city and therefore develop a blasé attitude, while the possibilities and even the constraints of individual freedom increase more than ever.[37] In a more abstract characterisation, Hasse argues that Simmel's main point is that the city dweller must develop an ability to live with the conditions of the city in a way that is adapted to their situation.[38] The big city gives rise to a certain way of life. "Urbanity" is the ability to live in and with the "chaotic diversity" that characterises the city, a diversity of impressions, environments and people. Urbanity is what arises in the very life of the city. The urban atmosphere is thus one that is not an atmosphere in its own right but consists of the mutual permeation and superimposition of several atmospheres; its essence is the plurality itself. As Hasse himself puts it: "The lived space of the city constitutes itself as a polyatmospheric world."[39] In the modern city, there are no obviously delimiting channels between the atmospheric islands of the neighbourhoods, but the borders themselves are fluid and dynamic, where the atmosphere of one neighbourhood affects the other and where a change in the atmospheric whole of the city, through a natural disaster or a major sporting event, for example, affects the atmosphere of the parts.

The city's atmosphere is polyatmospheric for many reasons. One of these is that the city offers institutionalised spaces for qualitatively very different atmospheres, which also vary in intensity in relation to each other. In previous chapters, I have focused on a few such spaces that differ

---

36    Hasse 2015b, pp. 37, 129, 146; Hasse 2015a, pp. 36, 88, 115.
37    Simmel 2002, p. 11.
38    Hasse 2015a, p. 79.
39    Hasse 2015a, p. 91.

atmospherically: the sports arena, the museum, the classroom, the home and the shop. But the city is also made up, albeit in different ways in different cities, of the square, the park, the cinema, the shopping centre, the town hall, the detention centre, the prison, the library, the concert hall, the temple (church, mosque or synagogue), the office complex, the restaurants, the cafés, the factory, the wasteland, the gardens and so on. What characterises the city is that all these spaces, which are more or less atmospherically different, are also very close to each other. It is thus not only possible but also common to immediately exchange one atmospheric space for another: after going to church, I immediately go to the gym and then go shopping for food before returning home. Or I go to a bar after work in my office and then continue to the cinema. In all these contexts, I am not only encountering different rooms, but I am also constantly encountering new and strange people in these different rooms. Being able to make all these changes of atmosphere (of more or less intense degrees) belongs to the experience of the urban atmosphere as such; the urban atmosphere belongs to all of the particular atmospheres together and not only to one or some of them.

Some of these spaces that belong to the urban space offer radically different ways of being from those accepted by society, a place of human desire that transcends the dreams that established society allows us to dream. It is these spaces that Michel Foucault calls "heterotopias", in other words "other places" or "counter-spaces", because they contrast with what is understood as regular spaces.[40] They can be religious or rather numinous spaces, as I will consider in the next chapter, but they can also be libraries, cinemas, clubs and gardens. Urban space is anything but homogeneous.

The perception of the urban atmosphere in its polyatmospheric form is fundamentally a question of existence, of being physically present in the urban space. If we can get an image of the atmosphere of a city through tourist brochures or travelogues, this is just an image and not the atmosphere as such, since its perception requires our concrete, bodily presence in the space.[41] Goethe got an image of Rome from the etchings hung in his childhood home, which were then replaced by the actual experience of the atmosphere of Rome once he travelled there. The image is the promise or hope of experiencing the atmosphere of the place, but one can be disappointed, surprised and reconciled, like Goethe. Again, as with architecture, there is often a kind of assumed oculocentrism in the notion

---

40   Foucault 1986, pp. 22–27.
41   Böhme 2013, p. 131.

that the sense of sight is our primary source of our impression of the city. But here, too, the urban atmosphere is a synesthetic and multimodal experience that cannot be reduced to a single or a few senses but concerns corporeality as such. The multimodal nature of corporeal existence, combined with the nature of the urban atmosphere as an agglomeration of atmospheres, makes it difficult to capture in writing or image the concrete atmosphere of a city.

The Parisian author Georges Perec (1936–1982) writes, "I like my town, but I can't say exactly what I like about it."[42] It is difficult, but not impossible, to say what it is, and there is consequently an established body of field research that examines the atmospheres of the city.[43] Perec does not find it impossible either, but his examples are anecdotal for good reason: "I love certain lights, some bridges, the outdoor cafés." To approach the question of what more concretely constitutes the city's atmosphere, I turn again to Hasse, using his list of ten concretisations (which he makes no claim of being complete) to illustrate how the perception of urban atmospheres is much more than visual impressions: building culture, smell, light and shadow, sound, air, rhythm, gaze, dress and habitus, the presence of animals and the presence of things.[44] Even if I treat some of them a bit more extensively than others, together they serve to clarify how complex the bodily experience of urban atmospheres (as well as the atmosphere of the home and basically all atmospheres) really is.

*Building culture.* It is certainly not surprising that building culture affects the atmosphere of a city. The architectural history that characterises an urban area immediately leaves its mark on the atmosphere. To use a clear example, we can recall the difference between walking in hyper-modern urban environments such as downtown Manhattan, Hong Kong or Tokyo, with their skyscrapers, walking in urban environments such as central Verona, Rome and Naples, where remnants of the ancient and medieval city are still present, and walking in neighbourhoods characterised by the uniformly designed modernist high-rise buildings of the 1960s in Rinkeby, Hammarkullen or Rosengård in Sweden. However, the atmospheric impact of building culture does not stop at architectural style but also is tied to how newer buildings relate to historic buildings (sedimentation or competition?), maintenance (is the decay of the buildings perceived as patina or just wear and tear?), colouring (Gothenburg's yellow brick versus Stockholm's ochre-coloured plaster facades) and so on. Paris changed

---

42    Perec 2008, p. 63.
43    Thibaud 2015a.
44    Hasse 2015b, pp. 216–223.

completely in physiognomy and atmosphere and became the Paris we now know when its medieval alleys were replaced by wide boulevards in Baron Haussmann's zoning project between 1853 and 1870.[45] The crucial insight is that a city's atmospheres are not primarily about building culture as an idea or opinion but about the experience of it for those who live in it and walk along its streets or indoor passages, as in many of the hypermodern urban environments.

*Odour*. The influence of smell on the perception of the city's atmosphere may be rarely mentioned in tourist brochures, but it is probably one of the most important atmospheric elements of the city. In an almost imperceptible way, it is possible to feel at home when you get off the train and the subliminally recognisable smells of your hometown hit you. The scent of the city has therefore, at least occasionally, been the subject of sustained attention by the authorities, such as in France at the end of the eighteenth century and later, when attempts were made to regulate and monitor smells in public spaces in a form of the deodorisation of society.[46] The cities of history probably offered what our time would perceive as a rather strong stench: in 1858, London experienced what is known as the "Great Stink" when untreated human and industrial waste on the banks of the Thames heated up in the hot weather; in the summer of 1880, Paris was plagued by a similar problem. Bad odours were seen as a direct threat to social order and eventually developed into a class marker. With the introduction of municipal sewers, cities' odour changed radically. Thus, there is reason to speak of the urban planning of that time as a disciplining of the cities' odours. Such discipline is justified not only by strictly hygienic reasons but also by an aesthetic perception of the social significance of odours. Our time does not share that era's pre-Pasteurian pathologising of bad smells, but that does not mean that smells, personal as well as more collective, have lost their significance for the atmosphere in the sense that the term is used in this text. One reason for the atmospheric importance of smells and the attempts to discipline them is that the sensation of smells is an enveloping and immersive experience; it is not easy to resist scents, and therefore they are beyond our active control. We must relate to them with this in mind. Unlike what we see, they have no "distance quality", which also explains their increasingly widespread commercial use: many shops as

---

45    Christiansen 2018.
46    Courbin 1982.

well as hotels and, increasingly, cities have a very conscious and calculated olfactory design.[47]

*Light and shadow*. New York, but also Paris and several other cities, can claim to be the "city of light" in several senses: the metaphorical reference to the city of enlightenment is superimposed onto the more concrete visual of the city of illumination. Light art, annual Christmas displays and illuminated esplanades use light to set the mood. But light and shadow play an important role in the atmosphere of the city in more ways than as a potential mood element or as a metaphor for enlightenment and modernity. In the city, functioning street lighting is important for the experience of safety. Monica Sand has shown how lighting is a recurring focus in art projects based in neighbourhoods in Sweden that were built under the so-called Million Programme. In the district of Tynnered in Gothenburg, the issue was addressed directly through artwork that served to light up the road to the community centre.[48] This solved a practical problem of poorly maintained street lighting in the area, though the problem was not only practical but also symbolic: the poor maintenance of the street lighting not only meant insecurity for those who had to move around in the dark; it also symbolised the alienation experienced by the inhabitants of the suburb. The absence of functioning street lighting is therefore a matter of both concrete and metaphorical shadowing, and it becomes a matter of atmosphere through both darkness and social deprivation.

*Sound*. Every city, if not every neighbourhood, has a soundscape that gives the space its distinctive character. Again, these areas include a variety of impressions: car traffic, the squeaking of trams on the rails, the cry of seagulls, sound signals at pedestrian crossings, the wind blowing in the trees, the morning rush in the underground corridors of the subway, street musicians, people shouting at each other and cars honking. As an advert I saw for a bagel shop in Chicago once claimed, the same bagels as in New York but without the honking and the swearing. The soundscape that characterises a particular city or neighbourhood is the one that arises and takes place in and through all of the urban sounds found in it. But often the sounds of the city remain only as a vague background or auditory scenery, except when particular circumstances make a sound intrude or we are particularly sensitive to it. Jean-Paul Thibaud cites the nocturnal walk as an example of when our sense of hearing is sharpened to otherwise anonymous sounds: "The nocturnal walk opens our ears to two main sources of our

---

47    Hasse 2015a, p. 89.
48    Sand 2019, p. 111 *et passim*.

intimate noise: breathing and the step."[49] If I then suddenly hear quick steps behind me, the sound itself becomes a form of localisation. Similarly, other sounds can also become the object of our attention, emerging from their anonymity for a moment. However, our everyday inattention to city sounds risks reducing them to noise. Instead, the specific soundscape of the part of the city where we feel at home is a soundscape that we recognise in an intuitive, preconscious way and is an integral part of the neighbourhood's atmosphere. We identify places, seasons, and times of day through the sounds of the city. Like smells, sound is an immersive experience that lacks the distance quality of the sense of sight and thus becomes one of the most important elements in the atmospheric experience of the city.

*Air.* What is the air in a city like? Is it affected by car exhaust and factory emissions? Is there a risk of inversion, where exhaust gases and pollutants cannot leave the ground level and cause problems for the city's inhabitants? Is the city close to the sea, like Gothenburg, so that wind and humidity have a greater impact than in Uppsala, for example, and therefore become part of the experience of the harbour or coastal city? Air is a factor in the city's atmosphere that relates to conditions in the city and its traffic and pollution, but also in its geographical location and its climatic conditions. Air can be experienced as high and clear but also low and oppressive; it can be cold and dry as well as hot and humid in ways that have a significant impact on the experience of the city's atmosphere. High-pressure air is associated with a rising mood, while oppressive, low-pressure air is associated with a falling mood.[50] How buildings relate to the street affects the air in a way that can be more or less hospitable. Air is, of course, intimately associated with our breathing, and its atmospheric meaning therefore combines both the symbolic and the concrete physicality of breathing.

*Rhythm.* Rhythm is about movement in the city, about tempo, about the pulse of the city. Moving from a hypermodern city like New York to a smaller city like Stockholm results in a more or less conscious sense of how the rhythm changes. A big city is said to be characterised by a fast pace, by a pulse, but at the same time the sheer number of people moving on Fifth Avenue in Manhattan on a December day can bring the pedestrian traffic to a sudden stop on the sidewalk. For a beat, no one gets anywhere. Further, rhythm is not only about people's movements on their own but also in relation to car traffic, public transport and so on. That a modern city should have a high tempo or fast rhythm is almost an atmospheric matter

---

49    Thibaud 2015a, p. 82.
50    For further elaborations about this, see Bachelard 1988.

of course, but at the same time the experience of rhythm is relative to habit. Stockholm author Stieg Trenter provides the following observation on traffic at Slussen:

> The clocks in Gamla Stan had just struck five, and endless cavalcades of cyclists and cars flowed through the multitude of lanes, split up, disappeared under grey viaducts, and reappeared in the bright afternoon light. The huge roundabout was a seething cauldron.[51]

Anyone reading this on a visit to Beijing in the spring of 2019, for example, and realising that Trenter's novel was published in 1945 and depicts a traffic situation taking place in that time period might wonder whether the atmospheric sense of rhythm in the city is not relatively constant as long as one does not compare it with other cities and other times. However, rhythm is not just speed but opens up a number of aspects of how we move around the city, particularly the proxemic competence of how to move around the city without bumping into other people, things or traffic. The nature of a taxi journey in Naples is very different from a taxi journey in Stockholm. In addition to the rhythm of the city, we can look at its choreography.

Hasse, as I mentioned, also talks about *gazes*, an idea that addresses both how people in the city actually look at each other and about the opportunities to look at each other that it offers. This is an important issue in terms of urban power. *Dress and habitus*, as Simmel taught us, express a specific urban way of life adapted to the rapid changes of the city. The *presence of animals* plays a role in the atmospheric experience of the city, whether they are animals we consider native to the city, such as pigeons and cats, or those we think of as invasive, such as foxes and elks. The *presence of things* is about how we use different things in the city and how things become class markers. In short, together these elements of our experience form what Thibaud calls "the sensory fabric of urban atmospheres".[52] As we move through the city, perhaps on foot, our sense of the urban atmosphere is the bodily experience of all these elements. Some may be more intrusive while others, due to our habit or their low-key nature, do not quite reach a conscious level but remain subliminal. However, sensing an urban atmosphere is not a matter of focused attention, although it is always possible to select individual elements for special attention. For example, the odour of the city may irritate me. I can make

---

51    Trenter 1945, p. 74.
52    Thibaud 2015b, pp. 203–215. More expansive in Thibaud 2015a, pp. 177–237.

a sound installation to become more aware of the sounds that are heard in the city but which are usually reduced to a backdrop. The stately streets of Vienna impress me with their width and length. The architectural interplay between the national romanticism of Engelbrektskyrkan, the brutalism of the old Arkitekturskolan and the facades of Lärkstaden in Stockholm forms a beautiful chord. But essentially, the experience of urban atmospheres is an experience of a "chaotic multiplicity" that is a whole before it can be divided into different elements. The experience of urban atmospheres is like the diver's experience of water: enveloping and engulfing, even if we do not drown in it.

In our time, there are ever-present political ambitions to plan and stage a certain atmosphere in the city through iconic buildings designed by star architects, a beautified city centre and the entertainment industry. But the urban atmosphere can only be planned to a certain extent. The chaotic diversity that makes up the city's urban atmosphere is an effect of factors that are beyond human control even if they are produced by humans. The developer or urban planner relates to the city in a different way than the pedestrian or bus passenger, namely as project and product rather than as process and environment.[53] Although both urban planning and walking in the city contribute to its dynamics, it is the walker who stages its urbanity through the concrete use of the city. Even the developer and the urban planner are, at the end of the day, people who live in the city and become part of the chaotic diversity that gives rise to its atmosphere. "Urbanity cannot be rationalized", writes Hasse.[54] One reason for this, besides the chaotic diversity, is the historical aspect: atmosphere is a consequence of urban sedimentation or how we engage with history. Trying to reinvent a neighbourhood or start from scratch always risks demolishing all the memories embodied in brick, stone and wood that make the city a place just for us, a place we recognise because of and thanks to our use of it and its atmospheric charge. The city, like the home, is a way of turning a space into a place and thus, if not controlling, at least cultivating atmospheres in a way that makes them liveable. Like with Schmitz's idea about the home, the city, through the limits it always has, also becomes a way of managing atmospheres.

---

53    Hasse 2015b, pp. 206, 208, 235.
54    Hasse 2015b, p. 185.

## Nature

When Antoine de Saint-Exupéry describes the desert, the night and the stars in *Southern Mail*, it is a literary attempt to reproduce an atmosphere of peacefulness. In the case mentioned by Saint-Exupéry, it is evident that human beings are not the producers of the atmosphere: not desert nor night nor stars depend on our human ability to exist. Here, unlike in the home or in the city, we encounter something genuinely different, something that does not belong or is taken from our own human potency. Of course, the atmosphere itself is not independent of the presence of people (and, perhaps, animals?) who experience it. But unlike, for example, the atmosphere of the home, where we ourselves, like the architect and builder of the house, very concretely contribute to the creation of a certain atmosphere, it is not we who produce the desert, the night and the stars, which constitute the very conditions for this atmosphere of peacefulness. In Chapter 2, with the help of Böhme, I made a distinction between atmospheres and the atmospheric, where the atmospheres are dependent on us as co-producers, while the atmospheric is at a greater distance from the self.[55] The fact that the desert, the night, the stars and other natural phenomena are examples of the atmospheric means that there is something uncontrollable about them that escapes any attempt on our part to manage them. The desert is often understood in Western history as "a manifestation of the Absolute".[56] This has to do with its contrast with the complexity of the lifeworld as well as with the fact that it provides us with no existential foothold. For Saint-Exupéry, the desert represents a limit to human action; once in the desert, there is little to do but surrender to its potential benevolence. We can certainly make a home there, but it is largely on the desert's own terms. Atmospherically, the desert is related to the sublime, the numinous but also the uncanny.

The home and the city can both be understood as attempts to manage atmospheres by enclosing a space that allows us to live with them constructively. Just as the roof that protects against rain must not be understood as a denial of nature, there is no intrinsic value in constantly allowing the atmospheric to overwhelm us. As such, the boundary has a humanising function, in that it gives form to space. The historic city was often demarcated by a physical boundary in the form of a wall. Even if our own time has not done away with the wall as a border – think of the Berlin

---

55    Böhme 2001, p. 46. Cf. pp. 46–71.
56    Norberg-Schulz 1980, p. 45.

Wall or the wall between Israel and Palestine – the practical disappearance of the city wall does not mean that the city is without borders, physical but also economic, political, social and even ethnic and religious. Added to this is also the demarcation with nature. Without boundaries with nature we probably cannot live, but even these boundaries can turn into a neurotic need for control that develops into an antagonistic relationship with the natural world. Our own age is sometimes called the Anthropocene in an attempt to characterise this need for control, where humans are influencing nature in a way that threatens geology, climate, environment and the biosphere. The boundary between city and forest has not only resulted in humans becoming more and more alienated from the forest, but also, and perhaps most importantly, the forest is increasingly allowed to grow only on human terms, and the area of the globe covered by forest is gradually shrinking. The desert as well as the forest are atmospherically related to the sublime, the numinous and the uncanny, and the attempt to deal with atmospheres can sometimes turn into a kind of immunisation against atmospheres, at least those that cannot be controlled and tamed.

At a time when humankind has largely subjugated nature, nature manifests itself mainly through the seasons, weather and wind. We feel the cloudy and humid November weather, the sultry weather before the thunderstorm, the seductive spring atmosphere, the powerful and dry cold of a fresh and sunny winter morning. These are natural phenomena we have not yet managed to tame, despite our climate impact. If, in the Anthropocene, humans delimit themselves *from* nature by trying to control it, these natural phenomena are about encountering nature *as* a boundary in the form of the uncontrollable. Here the seasons and the weather remind us of the desert and the forest, and for that matter the sea and space, in their uncontrollability, although the desert, forest and sea are subject to constant attempts at control. When Böhme writes about what he calls an "ecological aesthetics of nature", it is about a different way of relating to the natural world than through alienation and antagonism. Nature here stands for what cannot be disposed of, the "nonidentity in things under the spell of universal identity", to quote Theodor Adorno.[57] Beyond Adorno, however, Böhme seeks a reconciliation with nature in the realisation that a human being themself as a corporeal being is part of it.

In a reconciled relationship with nature, people are not only productive but also receptive. We experience the bodily presence in our environment through our existence. It is therefore not a question of judging nature

---

57    Böhme 1989, p. 19; Adorno 1997, p. 73.

aesthetically or depicting it but of experiencing it as an atmosphere through all our senses and the way it affects us. The aesthetics of nature that Böhme advocates for is thus, as we have already seen, an *Aisthetik* – a theory of sensory perception and not just a philosophy of art – that concerns how we are present in our environment. Here the human being is not seen as someone who is only active in relation to nature but as someone who is primarily affected *by* nature, affectively as well as physically. In relation to nature, living in atmospheres means living in an environment that set a limit to human activity and production. Böhme emphasises that humans are dependent on nature for their production.[58] As something perceptible, nature becomes a partner to human sensory experience, and we become its co-producers. But doesn't a one-sided emphasis on the relationship of dependence risk overlooking how nature also sets limits for humans? Böhme also writes that nature has an independent existence and that a human being "does not want to live in a world where he only encounters himself", which suggests that nature has autonomy from humans.[59] But the garden remains the ideal rather than the forest for Böhme, or, in other words, processed nature is more desirable than unprocessed nature, in a time when humanity's domination of nature seems increasingly inevitable.[60] Böhme speaks of a renaissance of the natural beauty, but in experiences of the sublime, numinous and uncanny, it becomes clearer how nature sets a limit to all our human attempts to separate ourselves from it. It calls into question all our claims that the initiative in any relationship with nature comes from us. Another way of putting it is that there is an atmospheric expressivity to nature as such, but not necessarily as an expression directly addressed to us humans.

If the atmosphere of nature, in its various guises, constitutes an atmosphere in some sense independent of human will, there are also atmospheres that exist on the threshold of our human settlement in the home or the city. These correspond to various concrete forms of overlap between culture and nature: the garden, which I have already mentioned, but also the more or less wild animals that make the city their habitat, such as deer, foxes and wild boars, as well as the old buildings covered by vegetation, abandoned wastelands or garden houses.[61] The boundary between city and nature, like the boundary between the home and its surroundings, is a porous membrane whose permeability may vary but never seals tightly. Even if a

---

58   Böhme 1989, p. 74.
59   Böhme 1989, p. 92.
60   Böhme 1989, pp. 94–95.
61   "Ville sauvage" 2022; Hasse 2015b, pp. 266–275.

glass dome could turn the city into an urban greenhouse, such a city would not be self-sufficient but would depend on communication and exchange with the outside world. How then should we understand this border as a porous membrane from an atmospheric perspective?

For Böhme, the garden is "socially constituted nature", and gardening is the art of "producing nature as nature".[62] For him, gardening means a humanisation of nature. He finds the roots of such an ideal in everything from the stories of paradise, the Garden of Eden, to the English gardening of the eighteenth century to today's ecological thinking. The difference between English and French gardening is the difference between trying to cultivate in accordance with nature and being antagonistic to nature. In English gardening, to which Böhme mainly relates, the gardener works *with* nature, and the ideal is that nature should assert itself through its cultivation. The relationship between gardener and garden in this case becomes a kind of alliance. The aim is to organise the garden in such a way that it evokes specific atmospheres of various kinds. According to the garden theorist Christian Hirschfelt (1742–1792), these are happy, gently melancholic, romantic and solemn gardens.[63] He presents a rudiment of an ecological aesthetic of nature, where we learn to live in and with nature in an age characterised by the irreversible impact of humanity on nature. Robert Pogue Harrison, in a cultural and historical discussion about gardens, has asked what kind of relationship between humans and nature is implied by the art of gardening. Gardening not only does something to the garden but also to the gardener. Gardens are no place for a triumphant attitude towards human production. Instead, gardening is a form of humble care, in which the gardener, precisely through his work with the garden, marks his or her special position in relation to the garden, while at the same time coming ever closer to it through constant attention to its growth. We can recall here the typological distinction between the engineer and the craftsman from the previous chapter. Gardening is a form of human cohabitation with nature. But even if gardening is a form of human agency, the claim that humans *create* the garden is not true. What we are doing is *cultivating* the garden, turning nature into culture, and thus putting our relationship with nature in order rather than ordering nature as such. The cultivation of a garden then has a somewhat different character than the act of making a space into a home or a place because the garden as nature is a clearer counterpart to the human being than the physical space. Even in

---

62   Böhme 1989, p. 92. Cf. pp. 79–95.
63   Böhme 1989, p. 89.

our cultivation of the garden, nature has a life of its own that takes place independently of this cultivation: "The flower confronts us with a beauty that exists independently of the human will – a beauty that we cannot create but only cultivate in our garden."[64] The gardener's relationship with their garden can be characterised as mediopassive: an attempt to make use of the life that sprouts in the garden. Gardening is therefore characterised by patience and hope as an existential disposition; the gardener must wait for nature's own initiative and practice their art as a response rather than an initiative.

In the gardens around Versailles, a high-profile example of French gardening, Harrison sees a parade of human arrogance in the attempt to subjugate nature.[65] These gardens are strictly oculocentric. Here humans' relationship with nature becomes antagonistic, unlike the gardening that Harrison himself advocates for, which is about the gardener being physically present in the garden and working *with* it. What emerges more clearly here than in Böhme is nature's own initiative in the garden, that there is a life force independent of human intention.

In the forest, which according to Harrison in Western history "represents an outlying realm of opacity", this trait of independence becomes even more evident.[66] In the garden, when it allows itself to be cultivated, nature gives itself to us, but in the forest nature shows another side: its sovereign indifference to human initiative and human benefit. If the cultivation of the garden represents a humanisation of nature, the forest represents a limit to this humanisation, which is also latent in the garden, though not to the same extent as in the forest. Of course, those who live at the edge of the forest can claim to know the forest better than the city dweller, and the archipelago dweller can likewise claim to know the sea better than the landlubber from the city. The boundary does not begin abruptly at the edge of the forest or the sea. The forest can be both home and workplace, as can the sea.[67] At a time when there is almost no forest left unaffected by human purposes, it is essential to find a way of relating to the forest that is similar to that of the gardener. But somewhere, even for the forester or fisherman, the familiar stops and the unfamiliar takes over. If nature, in the forest but also in the desert, the sea or space, represents an outer limit to humanity's attempt to

---

64    Harrison 2008, p. 47. See also Mallgrave 2022 for a discussion of architecture and gardening.
65    Harrison 2008, p. 113.
66    Harrison 1992, p. xi.
67    Solnit 2005.

subjugate our environment, its atmospheres of sublimity, numinosity or uncanniness are an affective reminder of this limit.

It is through the recognition of living in such atmospheres, impossible to reduce to human production, that it also becomes possible to live with atmospheres. As mentioned, the question of atmospheres is not just about atmospheres in isolation but about how we understand the relationship between human beings and the world, including the relationship between humanity and nature. Is it we who take the initiative in those relationships, or is our activity mainly a response to something we first receive? From an atmospheric perspective, the answer is the latter.

# 6.
## Numinous Edifices

In this penultimate chapter, I will explore the experience of the sacred with a focus on how it is realized in and through spatial categories, particularly buildings. My aim is to show how this experience is an aesthetic experience – "aesthetic" as laid out in Chapter 2, as an examination of the knowledge of our world gained intuitively and through our senses. At the same time, this chapter touches upon a number of themes that we already have encountered in previous chapters, such as the experience of overwhelming atmospheres as well as the relationship between the receptive and the productive aspects of atmospheres. I suggest that the experience of the sacred in sacred buildings is exemplary for both of these inquiries, as it highlights the irreducible externality of atmospheres, as Schmitz suggests in his lament of the lack of interest in Rudolf Otto in the phenomenological tradition – Otto being one of his allies against the introjectionists.[1] Here, I am mostly interested in how the sacred is experienced, not in whether it should be interpreted as an apprehension of the divine or some supramundane being. At the same time, I am also concerned with uncovering some of the shortcomings in how phenomenology has treated the topic, especially concerning the relationship between the power and the performance of the sacred as well as the sometimes quite abstract and generalizing talk of the sacred in some classic accounts.

Regarding terminology, I use sacred and numinous more or less as synonyms, which I believe is generally the case in the literature, although I have some sympathy for Rudolf Otto's understanding of the numinous as the sacred minus the moral. My exploration shall proceed with a critical look at some of the classic contributions on the topic; we may well have reservations about some of their suggestions, but to dialectically proceed through them may have the constructive advantage of clarifying their shortcomings while building on their strengths in the service of a revised understanding of sacred spaces. At the end, I offer

---

1     Schmitz 2019a, pp. 74–75.

some constructive suggestions on how to improve the way in which we deal, phenomenologically, with numinous edifices. But let me start with a short stroll to some of Rome's more illustrious examples of numinous edifices.


*Strolling Through Rome*

Once, when I was strolling through the Centro Storico in Rome, sometime after the third wave of the coronavirus, I was struck by the long queue for the Pantheon. Usually, one can simply walk straight through the portico into the rotunda, but at this time, no doubt because of the health measures called for by the pandemic, one had to stand in line to get in. Judging by the length of the queue, the wait did not seem to deter the visitors: the Pantheon remained one of Rome's best-attended monuments. Although I usually take the time to visit this site whenever I am in Rome, this time I decided to pass. However, a few days later I went to St. Peter's Basilica, avoiding the longer queues by arriving early in the morning. At 8:30 am, the queues for the security and health checks were short, but soon, even the massive St. Peter's started filling up. Security checks were, to be sure, in place even before the pandemic, but it is still interesting to note how popular a visit to this monument is, despite the inconvenience of the security check.

No doubt there are many significant differences between the Pantheon and St. Peter's in terms of history, purpose and architecture, the first being (re)built as a temple by the Roman emperor Hadrian with the help of the architect Apollodorus of Damascus and dedicated around 126 CE and the second being (more or less) completed in 1626 as the most important church of Western Christendom. The Pantheon was, at least in the beginning, a sanctuary for Roman religion but was converted into a Christian church by Pope Boniface III in the seventh century and still functions, occasionally, as a church, even though it is the property of the Italian government.

What they share, and the reason that I mention them together here, is the experience of space that they both conjure up in the visitor. To enter the Pantheon's dome between the columns via the vestibule is a short, horizontal walk that abruptly ends with a vertical shift when our attention is drawn upwards in accordance with the central axis of the building. Our eyes are almost inevitably attracted to the *oculus* or eye in the centre of the dome, which is where the light enters from above. It is always open. The centre of gravity in the relationship between visitors and the space circumscribed by the edifice shifts from us to the temple as our own activity is transformed into a more passive receiving of the light that flows from the *oculus*. It is as if the eye in the ceiling is looking at us rather than we at it.

Something similar could be said of the experience of visiting St. Peter's. Arriving, as we do as unofficial visitors, from the Piazza San Pietro, we are enclosed by the colossal colonnade, designed four columns deep by Bernini as a forecourt of the basilica.[2] Although the square is, in itself, awe-inspiring, even in its horizontal direction towards the entrance of the basilica, the trajectory turns upwards after the entrance, as we are is struck by the vastness of the space circumscribed by the building. The dome of St. Peter's is 136.57 metres tall, compared with the Pantheon's 43.3 metres, and is one of the tallest domes in the world. The central nave that stretches towards the apse is 186.36 metres long and is lavishly furnished in a baroque style and ornamented with huge pilasters. The experience is overwhelming, not least due to the sheer volume of the space enclosed by the building. If the experience of space in the Pantheon, particularly the shift in the centre of gravity experienced by the visitor to the temple or from horizontality to verticality, could be described as intense, at and in St. Peter's, the similar shift in the centre of gravity is experienced as prolonged and massive. It is difficult to take in the vastness of St Peter's. Perhaps it is better experienced in a crowd, as a collective experience?[3] Like all the grand churches of European Christendom, it is not exactly a serene place of meditation but, rather, a crowded and cluttered place.

Here I am trying to conjure up some basic aspects of the experience of numinous spaces. The examples I have chosen are, of course, examples of temples (from the Latin *templum*), that is, places for worship of the divine. In fact, the Pantheon once was a sanctuary for all the gods (*pan* in Greek meaning "all" and *theion* "gods") and only later became a Christian church. We may perhaps even presume that one reason for turning the Pantheon into a Christian church was that the experience of numinosity remained, even for those inhabiting a post-Constantine Rome that had become Christian and that had a constrained relation to its non-Christian past. Undoubtedly there is a difference between entering the Pantheon in its pre-Christian days and entering after it had been redecorated more in accordance with Christian beliefs, but nevertheless its fundamental axes remain, and so also the possibility of experiencing the shift in the centre of gravity. This is an experience that is possible to have outside any traditional

---

2    Cf. Snickare 2012, pp. 65–83.
3    Cf. Gumbrecht 2020.

religious affiliation, often witnessed by visitors writing from an admittedly non-confessional perspective. I would even venture to suggest that this is a large portion of the attraction for the contemporary tourist. Standing in the queue, waiting to have their Green Pass checked, the expectation of a numinous experience is invoked by the space of the building. William L. MacDonald, in his book on the Pantheon, thinks the experience is "neither sacred nor secular" but goes on to describe it in terms that describe precisely such a crossing of the horizontal and vertical as an experience of the sacred does.[4] Such experiences are, of course, coloured by one's religion or lack thereof. However, I suggest that neither religion nor personal belief is the cause of these experiences but, rather, that they are a function of space itself or, perhaps better stated, they are the relationship between human beings and a particular kind of space, defined by a certain kind of building. The experience of numinous space is the experience of an embodied being who, due to the embodied nature of their existence, is always also a spatial being.

### *Mircea Eliade's Sacred Space*

The common denominator and point of departure for a phenomenological discussion of what I call numinous or sacred spaces is likely to be found in Chapter 1 of the Romanian historian of religion and philosopher Mircea Eliade's classic *The Sacred and the Profane: The Nature of Religion*, written in French but originally published in a German translation in 1957.[5] The chapter is entitled "Sacred Space and Making the World Sacred" and is a summary of the experience of space in several religions and what is common to them all. Eliade is keen to uphold the commonality of experiences of the sacred among all human beings throughout his book. In it, he is heavily dependent upon the binary distinction between sacred and profane, heterogeneity and homogeneity, cosmos and chaos, as well as centre and periphery. In Otto Friedrich Bollnow's *Human Space*, which we have come across several times already, there is a chapter on sacred space that is essentially based on Eliade's account, with the addition of a few pages from the Dutch historian and philosopher of religion Gerardus van der Leeuw's *Religion in Essence and Manifestation* as well as from a

---

4    MacDonald 1976, p. 132.
5    Eliade 1959, pp. 20–65.

few other authors such as Hans Sedlmayer and Ernst Cassirer.[6] I take my current point of departure from a critical reading of Eliade's book, so let me begin with a short summary of what it says.

Eliade's chapter on sacred space begins with the distinction between heterogeneous and homogeneous space. The experience of a certain space as sacred is an experience of that space as different from other spaces. Space in its most general form is experienced as a vast expanse without any form; only the hierophany, the manifestation of the sacred, establishes a centre around which orientation is possible. In this way, a world is established where qualitative distinctions are possible. "There is, then, a sacred space, and hence a strong, significant space; there are other spaces that are not sacred and so are without structure of consistency, amorphous", writes Eliade.[7] The founding of the world *is* the differentiation within space between sacred and profane. For the non-religious human being or the human being without any notion of the sacred, space can only appear as undifferentiated, amorphous and neutral and, like the scientific geometrical space, without existential significance. However, this is only possible in theory, according to Eliade, not in practice, as some kind of "valorization of the world" always remains, like "privileged places".[8] Only the founding of the world through a hierophany permits a true orientation in the world, and so, despite Eliade's quite obvious critique of industrial society for its levelling of human existence, the distinction between heterogeneous and homogeneous space is ontological, not just historical.[9]

In more concrete terms, the distinction or even opposition between homogeneous and heterogeneous space could be illustrated by my example of St. Peter's in front of the Piazza San Petro in Rome. The door and the threshold between the church and the square indeed mark the continuity between these significantly different spaces, but most of all they mark a form of discontinuity, according to Eliade: "The threshold is the limit, the boundary, the frontier that distinguishes and opposes two worlds – and at the same time the paradoxical place where those worlds communicate, where passage from the profane to the sacred world becomes possible".[10] This discontinuity is not a property of the threshold of a church door as such but holds both for thresholds in general (think of domestic thresholds that differentiate between the domestic and the public, as mentioned in the

---

6   Bollnow 2011, pp. 133–141; cf. Leeuw 1986, pp. 393–402.
7   Eliade 1959, p. 20.
8   Eliade 1959, pp. 23, 24.
9   Eliade 1959, p. 24.
10  Eliade 1959, p. 25.

previous chapters) as well as for other religious buildings, monuments and sites. Thresholds signify passage and transformation.[11] But entering a church or any other religious building is not the only way that this differentiation occurs. Within the religious building another opening usually occurs, where the sacred intervenes; this is the hierophany or theophany. This second opening need not occur each and every time, automatically as it were, but at least must be indicated by a sign or an evocation. Even if sacred space in one sense is a given, it is not static but has to be performed, though this performance is not, at least from the perspective of the sacred space, a construction of sacred space by human beings alone but "reproduces the work of the gods".[12] As Eliade puts it later, "every construction or fabrication has the cosmogony as [a] paradigmatic model".[13] This idea connects to my short description in the introduction of how our eyes turn upward towards the *oculus* when entering the Pantheon.

The heterogeneity of sacred space is not confined to particular religious buildings, sites or monuments. All the world could be a place of manifestation of the sacred, according to Eliade, and so with particular territories that are consecrated by a ritual. Since the distinction between the sacred and the profane *is* the origin of the world, any ordering of a previously unordered chaos is also a sanctifying act through which a cosmos is created. Eliade uses the erection of a Vedic fire altar as an example of how the claim for a new territory, whether through conquest or occupation, is a cosmogonic act through which what previously was, at least for us, an unordered chaos becomes part of "our world".[14] At least in archaic religions, according to Eliade, whatever world that is not ours is not a world but chaos: "the cosmicization of unknown territories is always a consecration; to organize a space is to repeat the paradigmatic work of the gods".[15] This works both ways: the loss of the token that signifies creation also undoes the cosmos, and with it, the community that belonged to that cosmos. The enemy that threatens one's own community is also a representative of chaos. Even the fortifications against enemies around a city are thus more than defences against human beings; circumscribing the city also rules out and holds off the powers of chaos.

For Eliade, the *axis mundi* or cosmic pillar through which all levels of existence commune with one another signifies the centre of the world.

---

11    See my work on thresholds, Sigurdson 2024.
12    Eliade 1959, p. 29.
13    Eliade 1959, p. 45.
14    Eliade 1959, pp. 30–31.
15    Eliade 1959, p. 32.

Now we are, in a sense, back to the sacred space in a more circumscribed meaning: the *axis mundi* could be manifested concretely in a religious building, site or monument. It need not be a building, like a church, as in my own introductory example; it could be a sacred mountain, like Meru in India or Fuji in Japan, or a city, like the former city of the emperor in Beijing (or the city of Rome, for that matter, or Jerusalem, or Mecca and so on).[16] This is where heaven and earth meet and where chaos is ruled out. It is the place that orders the world, the centre from which the world comes to birth, its navel.[17] Thus, the centre of the city or village symbolizes the creation of the world, and the centre of the city or village in a traditional society could be empty but could also be represented by a sanctuary. But more common dwellings like houses are also structured in the same way as are sacred buildings in that they, too, take part in the cosmic symbolism: "The house is an *imago mundi*".[18] Every house in that sense is a sacred space since it enacts and repeats the creation of the world by bringing order to space. That a certain space is considered sacred, such as a church or a mountain, does not exclude but presupposes that the entire world is sacred, and the former works rather as a representative of that more extensive sacred space, an intensification of it. According to Eliade, such buildings are derived from the primary experience of sacred space in its more extensive meaning, a sacred cosmos.[19] Sacred space as manifested in buildings is dependent on a particular, experienced worldview. At the same time, these buildings serve as a reminder of the sacredness of the cosmos and thus resanctify the world. Even if they are mere earthly versions of a more perfect transcendent ideal, they not only point towards their archetype but symbolically participate in it.

Finally, Eliade suggests that, on the one hand, for the "profane" human being in the modern world, there are no longer any distinctions that differentiate sacred from profane space, which means that such distinctions disappear. In the industrial age, when, for example, architect Le Corbusier suggests that a house is "a machine to live in", habitation becomes a matter of functionality only, and the distinctions between different kinds of habitation disappear and lose their cosmic significance.[20] Space becomes

---

16    Eliade 1959, pp. 38–39.
17    Eliade 1959, p. 44.
18    Eliade 1959, p. 53.
19    Eliade 1959, p. 58.
20    Eliade 1959, pp. 50, 56–57; the quotation from Le Corbusier 1986, p. 5. The introduction to Le Corbusier's book, originally in French from 1923, suggests on page 3 that this is more complicated than Eliade's mention in passing allows for:

homogeneous and dwellings, infinitely replaceable, as the desacralisation of the cosmos goes hand-in-hand with the desacralisation of human dwellings. On the other hand, Eliade thinks there are still vestiges of a more traditional worldview in industrial society. In the way that there are still rituals for settling into a new house, people still have "privileged places", such as where we are born or met our partner.[21] These are experiences of nonhomogeneous spaces, even though they lack any cosmic underpinning. It seems to me that Eliade is profoundly ambivalent about the possibility of experiencing a thoroughly profane space even by modern human beings, and perhaps, consequently, if profane space means homogenous space, then this is a space where no existential orientation is at all possible. Since even modern human beings do or must orient themselves, even existentially, then it seems to follow that the notion of a genuinely empty or homogenous space is more of a limit concept than anything encountered in practice.

## *Phenomenology in Eliade's Account of Sacred Space*

Eliade's understanding of sacred space is not just pure phenomenology in the sense of describing how space appears to human beings only as it appears in their experience. It is also ontological, in that it suggests what kind of "worldview" is implied by such experience. One could even get the impression that the worldview seems to take precedence, and, to be sure, Eliade never suggests that it is phenomenology that he is doing. Also, his account is highly abstract in that it generalizes from broad religious material, something Eliade himself admits by saying that it is not the infinite variety that interests him but, rather, the elements of unity. The emphasis on difference is between the two different attitudes of "religious man" and "nonreligious man".[22] Yet another characteristic of Eliade's interpretation of sacred space is that it abstracts from any actual description of how space is materially constituted and structured. It is hardly Eliade's point, I think, to dissociate material construction from existential significance,

---

"The Architect, by his arrangements of forms, realizes an order which is a pure creation of his spirit"; perhaps this is a creation of the architect's own spirit, and they now become the creator, but on the other hand, the architect "gives us the measure of an order which we feel to be in accordance with that of our world". Whatever the differences, it is remarkable how similar these accounts are in terms of the significance they ascribe to buildings.

21    Eliade 1959, pp. 57, 24.
22    Eliade 1959, p. 63.

even if he differentiates between "geometrical space" and the experience of heterogeneous space.[23]

Nevertheless, in effect Eliade leaves out from his discussion the possibility that the actual, material construction of space could give rise to genuine differences in the way that space is experienced existentially. Does the materiality of a building contribute to the way it is experienced, so that the tactile harshness of the concrete that the Pantheon is made of gives rise to a different experience than, say, the warmness of a wooden stave church? Do the different organizations of space in, for example, a traditional basilica, a gothic cathedral and a modern brick church with a flat roof bring about different conceptualities as well as experiences of how the divine is related to the created?[24] I suggest that Eliade's emphasis on elements of unity between different manifestations of the religious worldview and, especially, different instances of sacred architecture actually obscure some of the complexity of the experience of sacred space and how it is dependent on sense impressions.

Along with this tendency comes, not surprisingly, another problem that I have already hinted at: that worldview precedes ontology in Eliade's account of experience. While I think it is certainly permissible and even commendable to ask what worldview certain experiences imply and vice versa, I cannot escape the impression that Eliade's reduction of the possible attitudes to just two, "traditional" and "modern" or "religious" and "nonreligious", is too simplistic. This distinction goes hand in hand with the experience of space as heterogeneous and homogeneous, respectively, but it does not really hold up for Eliade himself, as he insinuates that space is never really experienced existentially as purely homogeneous. Implicit in Eliade's argument is that the "modern" attitude has as its consequence an impossible flattening of the experience of space, but in a certain sense Eliade, too, with his description of sacred versus profane space in *The Sacred and the Profane*, practices such a flattening. What if it is the poverty of the descriptions of space that obfuscates the heterogeneity of the experiences of space rather than a lack of the experiences themselves? It is understandable that Eliade writes the way he does in a book from the 1950s that wishes to speak to how its own context perceives itself, but it is perhaps less an attempt to stay true to the experiences of space and more a polemical piece that risks overstating its case. Eliade's account runs the risk that his more historical distinction between sacred and profane,

---

23    Eliade 1959, pp. 22–23.
24    Cf. Kieckhefer 2004; Kilde 2008.

as a result of secularization, overrides a phenomenological distinction between space as sacred, as in a temple, and as profane, as in a market. In the latter distinction, sacred and profane could be understood not as a binary opposition but as a functional differentiation within society. Such a functional differentiation may well conform to a traditional society in the way Eliade conceives it, as the differentiation between special, "red letter days" and ordinary days in the liturgical calendar does not exclude that the whole month, or year, is sacred.

Consequently, my critique of Eliade's understanding of sacred space in *The Sacred and the Profane* has to do with its lack of phenomenological precision. We need only look at a comprehensive description of spatiality as an existential category, as in Bollnow's *Human Space*, to understand how complex spatiality as such is and that "homogeneity" might be an imprecise designation even of something called profane space from a phenomenological perspective. But perhaps I am unfair to Eliade, given that he never claims to be doing phenomenology in *The Sacred and the Profane*? Let us therefore take a short look at the section on sacred space in Bollnow's book to see what he does with Eliade, while also glancing at how he uses van der Leeuw's short section on the same topic.

In *Human Space*, Bollnow starts from Eliade's distinction but remarks almost at once that we need to be more careful in distinguishing between the homogeneity of abstract, geometrical space and the homogeneity of profane space, as the latter is only homogeneous in relation to sacred space.[25] For Bollnow, non-homogeneity is a characteristic of "experienced space", "space as it is manifested in concrete human life", as such.[26] Only when experienced space is colonized by abstract, geometrical space would it assume a homogeneous character, but even that goes against the grain of experience. Today, "in these secular times", "the house of the human individual is still a sacred area", according to Bollnow, so there is a limit to secularization in the sense of emptying the human dwelling of all existential significance.[27] According to van der Leeuw, there is a proximity between house and temple in traditional society, and Bollnow traces the remaining sacrality of the dwelling back to its roots in "mythological thought".[28] In his association of the existential significance of the dwelling with religious thought, Bollnow is essentially in agreement with Eliade. No secularization in the sense of a complete rationalization and externalization of human life

---

25    Bollnow 2011, p. 135.
26    Bollnow 2011, p. 19.
27    Bollnow 2011, pp. 133, 134.
28    Bollnow 2011, p. 134; cf. Leeuw 1986, p. 395.

is possible. But at the same time, Bollnow is more nuanced than Eliade in terms of his phenomenology.

To begin with, Bollnow emphasises that there are different forms of sacred space, and, perhaps more importantly, with the help of van der Leeuw he points out how the manifestation of sacred space occurs as an internal differentiation within space. As van der Leeuw puts it, sacred spaces "have their specific and independent value" as "resting-places" in "universal extensity" and thus become not a "part" of this universal extensity but a "position".[29] In other words, sacred space might well be a kind of centre, with the help of which human beings can orient themselves in space. However, this does not mean that whatever parts of space are not "centre", not sacred but profane, are just amorphous homogeneous extensions. Quite the contrary: even peripheral space stands in a non-antagonistic relationship to central space. Still, there is a recurring antagonism in Eliade's exposition between sacred and profane that is explained more by his cultural criticism than his phenomenology. Bollnow essentially agrees with Eliade's idea that, as Bollnow himself puts it, "every building of a house is the establishment of a cosmos in chaos", but this act of separation that is constitutive of a world does not mean that profane space will forever be associated with chaos.[30] Building a house or, for that matter, founding a city is a repetition of the primordial act of creation, which also means that the house or the city in itself symbolizes the creation of cosmos. As examples of this, Bollnow picks up Eliade's report of a Native American tribe, the Austrian art historian Hans Sedlmayr's account of the symbolism of Byzantine churches as well as Plutarch's account of the foundation of Rome.[31]

Essentially, Bollnow is more interested in the sacrality of the house, of human dwellings, than in the more pronounced sacrality of religious buildings and sites and how their "paler, but still effective form" is a reflection of "a purer and more primeval".[32] This comparison, he suggests, helps us to understand how even in modern times (Bollnow's book was originally published in 1963), "in these secular times", building and dwelling in a house retain something of a sacred character: the experience of the dwelling as in some sense the centre of the world, the house as set apart from other spaces, the house as a realm of peace and the house as an image

---

29    Leeuw 1986, p. 393.
30    Bollnow 2011, p. 137.
31    Eliade 1959, p. 46; Sedlmayr 2001, p. 119.
32    Bollnow 2011, p. 140.

of the world.[33] On the last point, he quotes Gaston Bachelard and suggests that being at home in a house is the presupposition of being at home in the world.[34] Bollnow's interest, in other words, is more in the experience of the sacred in "ordinary" spaces than in traditionally "extraordinary" spaces, such as religious buildings.

Writing a comprehensive phenomenology of the human experience of space, Bollnow's aim is different from Eliade's in *The Sacred and the Profane*. It is a phenomenology of everyday dwelling. Nevertheless, we can see a convergence in how Bollnow suggests that the house retains some of the characteristics of a more traditional form of sacred space and that, therefore, the distinction between "traditional religious" and "modern secular" is far from absolute. However, even in his dependence on Eliade for his own analysis, he is quietly but distinctly critical of Eliade's conflation of a historical narrative of secularization and a phenomenological distinction between sacred and profane space. In Bollnow's own account, existential space, whether sacred or profane, would not be reduced to homogeneity, except as a matter of the colonization of the spatial aspects of the lifeworld by an abstract, geometrical understanding of space. While there are indeed, as Eliade suggests, social trends that threaten to mute spatial "resonance" – the possibility of standing in a living relationship to one's environment and not just regarding it as inanimate – and while some of these trends *may* be effects of a scientistic (rather than scientific) worldview, that does not mean human beings in general experience space as something amorphous, homogeneous and inert. Instead, the vocabulary for describing experiences of spatial significance in everyday life is reduced, is privatized and, in the worst case, assumes an uncanny quality.[35] To a certain extent, Bollnow presents a more nuanced phenomenology of sacred space, especially in his clarifications. At the same time, he leaves out some of the more extraordinary experiences of sacred spaces (not just religious buildings), which might be disadvantageous to his understanding of the sacred as such and also, by extension, to his account of the house.

---

33    Bollnow 2011, p. 141.
34    Cf. Bachelard 1994, pp. 4, 7.
35    Cf. Rosa 2020.

## The Power of the Sacred

One essential trait of Eliade's understanding of sacred space that is missing from Bollnow's discussion and perhaps tends to be overshadowed by other concerns in Eliade's own analysis is the power of the sacred, its overwhelming quality. To experience a space as sacred is to have some experience of a power that cannot be fended off but that imposes itself on the person. This corresponds to the hierophany in Eliade's account: "Every sacred space implies a hierophany, an irruption of the sacred".[36] The word "hierophany" comes from a combination of the Greek adjective *hieros*, "sacred", and the verb *phanein*, "to bring to light", "to reveal". The verb emphasizes the dynamic character of how the sacred imposes itself on the recipient. In my short description of visits to the Pantheon and St. Peter's in Rome, I point out how the experiences of these two buildings involved a shift in the centre of gravity from visitor to space. This is an example of how the quality of power in the experience of the sacred is manifested concretely in the very form and materiality of a building. In other words, there is an active or even performative quality in how the power of the sacred asserts itself. I shall return to this performative quality later, but in this section I will focus on the question of what kind of power inheres in the manifestation of the sacred, taking my cue from one of Eliade's predecessors who was also an important writer for Hermann Schmitz, Rudolf Otto.

Whatever the source of an experience of the sacred and the nature of the sacred itself, an essential quality of that experience is how it asserts itself with power. The experience of someone who finds themself in the grip of the sacred is sometimes described as "awe", "astonishment", or even "dread". A classic interpretation of such experiences is found in Rudolf Otto's *The Idea of the Holy* from 1917, which is mentioned by Eliade as the starting point of his own reflections on religious experience.[37] Unlike Eliade, Otto, a German theologian and scholar of religion, wants to uncover and isolate to make more distinct that aspect of the "holy" (or sacred) that goes beyond any moral goodness or epistemological cognition, which he calls the "numinous". "Numinosity" is an adjective coined by Otto himself, and he derives it from the Latin *numen*.[38] A particular characteristic of the numinous is that we cannot actively create it; the initiative, so to speak,

---

36    Eliade 1959, p. 26.
37    Eliade 1959, pp. 8–10.
38    Otto 1958, pp. 6–7.

is always on the side of the numinous itself, even when its reception is conditioned by the receiver. As Otto puts it, the numinous "cannot, strictly speaking, be taught, it can only be evoked, awakened in the mind".[39] This means, as Otto is eager to emphasize, that any reception or reaction of the subject experiencing it is dependent upon its being "objectively given"; even if the numinous cannot be described as such, it is experienced as something "which in itself indubitably has immediate and primary reference to an object outside the self".[40] The important point about the numinous is not that it is an object in any definable sense but that it is something external to the subject, which means that it also can impose itself on the subject receiving it. This is also why Otto chose to talk about it as *das ganz Andere*, the "Wholly Other".[41] Even when Otto speaks of the numinous as a noun, his intention is quite the opposite of objectification. The numinous quality of the numinous itself can be spoken or written about, but strictly speaking it can never be defined, only experienced.

The numinous is experienced in a complex way, as a *mysterium tremendum et fascinans*. That it is a mystery essentially means that we cannot have the numinous at our disposal. It imposes itself; it takes the initiative. The aspect of *tremendum* accentuates this distance between the numinous and the experiencing subject. A translation of *tremendum* would be "awe inspiring" to the point of "dread" or the "uncanny". Otto summarizes it as "absolute unapproachability".[42] To further highlight that this still is a phenomenon that overpowers any human ability, Otto also speaks of the experience of the numinous as *majestas* – "majestic" – as a qualification of *tremendum*. In the experience of being overpowered, being a mere creature before something that absolutely exceeds oneself, unapproachability takes upon itself an aspect of humility on behalf of the subject. A third and final qualification of the numinous alongside *tremendum* and *majestas*, mentioned by Otto, is "energy" or "urgency". This aspect further stresses the active nature of the numinous object, which is not indifferent but appears to have its own desire.

Even given these different aspects of the experience of the *mysterium tremendum*, this is only one side of the experience of the numinous. If *tremendum* speaks of the distance between the numinous object and the experiencing subject, there is also the almost opposite or at least contrastive pull of the *fascinans*. The mystery of the numinous object has an "element

---

39    Otto 1958, p. 7.
40    Otto 1958, p. 10.
41    Otto 1958, pp. 25–30.
42    Otto 1958, p. 19.

of daunting 'awefulness' and 'majesty'" and "something uniquely attractive and *fascinating*" which "combine in a strange harmony of contrasts".[43] Despite the aspects of awe or dread, in the experience of the numinous, we are also drawn towards it as an object of desire in its own right, not only for the sake of "salvation" or anything else that is pragmatically useful. "Longing", "solemnity", and the sheer dazzlement and excitement of the over-abundant nature of the numinous characterise the fascination that is also part of this experience. For Otto, all these aspects, both of the *tremendum* and of the *fascinans*, help us to understand the phenomenon of the power of the numinous. However, these experiences are still generalizations of something that cannot, in principle, be defined, and in Otto's discussion of them in *The Idea of the Holy*, they are presented as drawn from empirical material that is quite rich in its nuances. In keeping with the irreducibly transcendent nature of the numinous, he can only represent these experiences through "ideograms", which hint at rather than denote their referent.[44]

In the wake of Otto's interpretation of the power of the sacred, we can now approach the question that I asked at the beginning of this section, concerning the nature of the power of the sacred or numinous. The "object-like" quality of the numinous, its status as a "quasi-object", to use the terminology from Chapter 2, is a presupposition of that power, which perhaps becomes clear if the moment of surprise is accentuated in the awe-inspiring and overwhelming experience of the numinous. A constitutive part of the experience of the sacred is the asymmetry implied between the experiencing subject and the numinous object in which, as mentioned, it is the latter that takes the initiative and, in keeping with the uncontrollable nature of the experience, does so seemingly spontaneously. Inspired by Otto, Hermann Schmitz defines the numinous, in terms slightly different from the previous discussants, as that which, "for a human being seized by it at the time in question" and then and there possesses authority in the form of an "unconditional seriousness".[45] Schmitz praises Otto for his phenomenological insight that the phenomenon neither belongs on the side of subjective feelings nor appears as an object, even though he thinks that Otto falls short of his own insight due to his dualistic Kantian epistemology. Schmitz himself, however, suggests that the numinous is an atmosphere that unconditionally lays hold of the person.[46] Dwelling, in

---

43    Otto 1958, p. 31.
44    Otto 1958, p. 19.
45    Schmitz 2019a, p. 87.
46    Schmitz 2019a, pp. 81–82.

the most general sense of the term, is, as we have seen in Chapter 5, the human attempt to become familiar with an atmosphere of this kind through carving out a leeway or an area that relieves us of this unmediated exposure to its unconditional authority.[47] Building a temple – or any house for that matter – is an attempt to circumscribe the numinous, to make it somehow manageable and possible to live *with* rather than *before*.

Schmitz is helpful when it comes to understanding the nature of numinous power. On one hand, as we have seen, this power takes its expression in and authority from what he calls an unconditional seriousness. On the other hand, through the dwelling, this unconditional seriousness is mediated so that human beings do not encounter it raw. This mediation of the unconditional sounds as if it were a paradox, but, cognitively, I don't think it is. Rather, it refers to the ambiguity or perhaps duality of the experience of the numinous. Otto was, as we have seen, quite emphatic about the ambiguous quality of the experience, but here it is a matter of another ambiguity or duality, more like Moses in the story of Exodus 33:18–34:9, who asks to see the glory of God but only gets to see his back, since no one could see God's face and live. In other words, God's manifest presence is only presented to Moses indirectly. Analogically, the temple, as an example of the circumscribing dwelling, both presents and obscures the numinous in that it holds together the fact that it is not at our disposal and the hermeneutical insight that if it somehow engages us, it therefore must come within our reach. In other words, there must be both continuity and discontinuity in the aesthetic experience of the numinous for it to be experientially meaningful and even relatable.

In terms of power, this means that it is, at least in principle, possible to recognize the authority of the numinous, its overwhelming quality, while understanding how it is possible not to be directly seized by it. Take the tourist visiting St. Peter's: it is indeed possible, as a tourist, to recognize as well as experience something of its numinous quality while yet remaining a tourist, someone visiting the basilica for sightseeing purposes rather than worship. Perhaps some of the allure of a numinous space like St. Peter's, even for the tourist, who may well be a non-believer or an agnostic unconcerned with its religious meaning, is found in the potential numinosity of the building itself, experienced both as present and distant. That it is possible to experience an atmosphere such as the numinous as both present and distant in a particular building is explained by an understanding of the numinous such as Schmitt's, as it shows why the various degrees of

---

47    Schmitz 2019a, p. 213.

experienced intensity do not contradict the asymmetry in the relationship between the numinous and the experiencing subject. There is indeed a shift in the centre of gravity from horizontality to verticality, but there is still the possibility of reflexively relating to this very shift while also recognising it. This means, in turn, that the power of the numinous should be understood not in purely causal terms but, rather, as an "insisting" power, a power whose vertical authority is mediated horizontally. Phenomenologically speaking, it is experienced more as a kind of dance than as an encroachment in this intertwining of activity and passivity, of horizontality and verticality. Here I turn to the performative quality of the sacred experience.


*The Performance of the Sacred*

If the power of the sacred draws attention to the vertical moment of the numinous, the performance of the sacred similarly stresses the horizontal aspect. I have suggested that, perhaps, verticality and horizontality should dialectically be held together rather than be disconnected from each other. But before I return to this hypothesis, let me first present what I mean by the performance of the sacred from a spatial perspective. In my narrative introduction to this chapter, I presented a short sketch of what an experience of the numinous could be from a first-person perspective. One distinguishing feature of such an experience that I wanted to highlight is its dynamic quality. The shortest version of a description of such an experience is that it entails a shift in the centre of gravity from horizontality to verticality, but in practical terms the experience entails approaching the building, entering it, walking farther inside it and so on. In other words, the experience of the sacred is dynamic rather than static. As I have already made clear, it indeed involves a form of passivity on the part of the experiencing subject in that they undergo this experience due to some form of power outside themself. At the same time, however, the passivity is not absolute, as indicated by the narration of how this experience came about. It involves a dynamic transformation from one state to another, and so the relationship between passivity and activity is more complex and nuanced than an either/or relationship. More detailed reports of experiences of the sacred, especially reports involving buildings such as the Pantheon or St. Peter's, usually emphasise how iteration contributes to the sense of the sacred, either in the form of liturgy or ritual involving the buildings or just the thousands or millions of people who visit them, year after year. It is not just a matter of experiencing the sacred in and through the buildings but also of being aware of how they have been and are treated as sites of the sacred.

In a well-known critique of Eliade and his discussion of sacred spaces, Jonathan Z. Smith has pointed out how sacred spaces are created by religious traditions, not just given as such. In *To Take Place: Toward Theory in Ritual*, Smith takes Eliade to task for privileging "event" before "memorial" and "cosmogony" before "politics" in religious history.[48] As Smith puts it, "there is nothing inherent in the location of the Temple in Jerusalem. Its location was simply where it happened to be built".[49] People made an active choice to build it where it was built; the location was not a necessity that passively had to be accepted, even though it was legitimated as such afterwards. Other places, of course, could have a necessary locative specificity, such as Bethel for its association with the patriarch Jacob (cf. Gen. 28:10–22). Even then, the associations of the place will be built through narrative and ritual. Thus, sacredness is more a matter of the use of a certain building or site than of any inherent properties in it: sacred power is situational rather than substantive.[50] Smith argues, "Ritual is not an expression of or a response to 'the Sacred'; rather, something or someone is made sacred by ritual".[51] This means that nothing is sacred in itself, nor is anything profane in itself. In other words, he states, "ritual is a means of performing the way things ought to be in conscious tension to the way things are".[52] Sacrality does not inherently dwell in certain spaces, even though experience might make it seem so; on the contrary sacrality is projected on certain spaces as an effect of rituals being performed in and around them. Sacred spaces are made, not found. The power of the sacred is a function of the horizontal, the temporal, and not of the vertical.

No doubt Smith's critique of Eliade (who actually mentions performance but does not offer any detailed account of it) is an important reminder that sacred spaces are always sites of power, where power is contested. Iteration is certainly a means for making a particular sacred space appear as if it were absolute and natural rather than relative and construed. As Smith points out, the history of religions is full of examples of how a particular place is imbued with new meaning through a ritual occurring there. There might be several reasons for speaking of "sacralised space" rather than "sacred space" to highlight this performative aspect of the

---

48    Smith 1987, pp. 1–23.
49    Smith 1987, p. 83.
50    Smith 1987, p. 104.
51    Smith 1987, p. 105.
52    Smith 1987, p. 109.

sacred. However, if Smith's critique is taken as replacing a vertical and substantive understanding of the sacred with a horizontal and situational understanding (which I am not sure was his intention), then there is a risk of underestimating the power of the sacred – and by power, I mean here its "insistence". Even if this power is in some way a function of ritual, the experience of it can hardly be altogether reduced to some kind of active intention behind the ritual. If it were just a matter of ritual, the act would be understood as an arbitrary imposition on space, with space (and place) in itself inert and mute.

I repeat my contention that this is not how space in general is experienced, and especially not sacred space. The experience of the sacredness of a certain space includes an excess that in its manifestation cannot be reduced to anything self-produced. Its spontaneous and imposing power is experienced as something beyond human control. Any particular experience of space, including, of course, sacred space, could well be illusory, in thinking that space actively imposes itself upon us. But if all our experiences of the heterogeneity of spaces are false, then our alienation is without limit, which would seem to include also our theories of the performance of the sacred. If spaces cannot assert themselves, but all their significances are actively and exclusively produced by us, then such a theory of the performance of the sacred is as subjectivistic as a theory of the power of the sacred, such as Eliade's, is objectivistic. Would, then, an experience of anything "other" (even with a lowercase "o") be at all possible, or would every "other" be reduced to "the same"? Are we not, to the same extent as in Eliade's account, again encountering a perspective that takes leave of the material as "other" if spaces cannot affect us in ways that go beyond our use of them?

I am far from suggesting that this is what Smith wants to say, even though he has formulations that might sound like it. In his polemics against a substantive interpretation of the sacred, he is understandably emphasizing a situational interpretation. His interest is not the phenomenon of the sacred as such or in everyday life; rather, it involves how the sacred is interpreted in religious studies and how particular historical instances of it have been misconstrued. What if we, as I have already hinted, do not think of the horizontal as the alternative or opposite to the vertical but, rather, as the way in which the vertical asserts itself, as a kind of excess over and in the horizontal? If there is, as Smith asserts, a mediation of the unconditional, then the sacred could be understood not as a static relationship between the sacredness inherent in a building and the one perceiving it but as a dynamic mediation of something that takes place in between subject and object, as a kind of irreducible surplus.[53] To understand how this can come about, I shall now take a closer look at how performance might work in relation to the sacred.

A performance, according to Erika Fischer-Lichte, whose *The Transformative Power of Performance* (German original from 2004) is a modern classic, concerns "the transformation of the performance's participants"; it disputes the dichotomous division between subject and object and turns the spectators into participants.[54] Thus, performance is about presence rather than interpretation, and the presence in question is not something that exists "before" or "outside" the performance itself; presence "happens" and is perceived as a form of energy.[55] However, it is important not to understand this performance as an individual's experience. On the contrary, it is an embodied co-presence among, in the case of theatre, spectators and actors and, of course, the material scene of the performance. This also is true for the performance of a certain building, city or site: the experience of a sacred space like St. Peter's involves the material edifice as much as other visitors, be they tourists or celebrants.[56] A performance, in other words, is as much material as it is aesthetic, political or social if these are understood as differentiated from one another.[57] All these dimensions of existence are intertwined in performance, and through the performance, any static dichotomies between subject and object or meaning and materiality become dynamized. As Fischer-Lichte describes the performance, it enacts what she calls an "in-between" state, or a state of liminality.[58] This is also what Eliade as well as Fischer-Lichte herself describe as a threshold. As discussed above, thresholds enact and signify passage and transformation, and so do performances. Fischer-Lichte talks about a "destabilization of the self, the world, and its norms" in "the experience of the concerned subjects", and this is very much what takes place when the point of gravity shifts in the aesthetic experience of sacrality in the Pantheon or St. Peter's.[59]

Fischer-Lichte notices the similarities between performances understood as art and as ritual and that they often are intertwined, even though she ultimately wishes to hold them apart.[60] The distinguishing mark is that

---

53    Cf. Waldenfels 2012, pp. 353–412.
54    Fischer-Lichte 2008, pp. 16, 17.
55    Fischer-Lichte 2008, p. 98.
56    Fischer-Lichte 2008, pp. 75–137; cf. Fischer-Lichte 2012, pp. 87–97.
57    Fischer-Lichte 2008, p. 51.
58    Fischer-Lichte 2008, p. 174.
59    Fischer-Lichte 2008, p. 179.
60    Fischer-Lichte 2008, p. 91.

artistic performances take place outside a ritual or religious context. They do not refer to another world that might mitigate their physical impact or imbue them with meaning. This claim is somewhat dubious, given both Fischer-Lichte's emphasis on the inevitable intertwining as well as the self-testimonies of performance artists.[61] Nevertheless, she is aware of how close a performative presence comes to some notion of the power of sacrality as it makes an impact on those within the sphere of its radiance. She sometimes uses a theological vocabulary, as in performance as a "transfiguration" of the commonplace, or when she uses the metaphor "*theatrum vitae humana*" [the theatre of human life] in understanding the relationship between art and life.[62] Furthermore, in the last chapter of *The Transformative Power of Performance*, she speaks of the "reenchantment of the world".[63] She understands reenchantment as a "liberation from all endeavors to understand and the revelation of the 'intrinsic meaning' of man and things".[64] Again, despite her nearness to some understanding of the sacred, in this last chapter she distances herself from what she calls a "two-world theory" and suggests that performance is characterized by "self-referentiality", even as she recognizes the "transformational power" of performance.[65] We may ask if this self-referentiality of performance really does justice to the openness or porosity of the subject that experiences a performance. Given the instability of the demarcation between art and reality in performance, according to Fischer-Lichte's own understanding, how can performance be defined as something that, as such, excludes the possibility of experiencing what Otto calls the "Wholly Other"?[66] It seems to me that she applies a much too stark distinction between a traditional notion of the sacred and that kind of sacrality that takes place in artistic performances, and she sees the former's "two-world theory" through a simplified lens. If "aesthetic experience", a transformative experience of the subject concerned, could be applied to non-artistic as well as artistic performances, then how could the "Wholly Other" be excluded

---

61    See, for example, the self-biography of Marina Abramovic 2016, in which Abramovic quite explicitly refers to Tibetan Buddhism as a background to many of her performances.
62    Fischer-Lichte 2008, pp. 168, 205.
63    Fischer-Lichte 2008, pp. 181–207.
64    Fischer-Lichte 2008, p. 186.
65    Fischer-Lichte 2008, pp. 181–207.
66    Cf. Fischer-Lichte 2008, p. 200.

in principle? As she herself states, "the border turns into a frontier and a threshold, which does not separate but connects".[67]

As spatiality as such is also something that happens in performance rather than being a static *thing*, sacred space is performed, and it is through the very performance of the space that its sacredness takes place. When the sacred space is performed, it also lays claim to a certain authority over those present. But even though sacrality is in some way produced, much like presence, this does not mean that its production should be taken as the opposite of its reception. Hans Ulrich Gumbrecht uses the Eucharist as an example of this dialectic: "the celebration of the Eucharist, day after day, will not only maintain but intensify the already existing real presence of God".[68] In this account, the situational character of the Eucharist both holds together its presentation with its representation and also makes it uncontrollable in its impossibility to plan. Fichter-Lichte's interpretation of the performance of the sacred, as we may well call it, is quite helpful in understanding how it is possible to speak of the production of an experience of numinosity in built edifices without denying the possibility of a power of the numinous that goes beyond human intention. As Paul Ricœur has noted in a similar discussion, the interpretation of a founding tradition is a constitutive part of that very tradition; the performance of the sacred is part of the efficacy of the sacred: "between the sacrality of space and the act of habitation subtle exchanges occur".[69] Ricœur shows us, in a manner not that distant from Fischer-Lichte, that the performance and the power of the sacred need not be understood as each other's opposites but can be held in dialectical tension.


*The Experience of the Numinous as an Aesthetic Experience*

Let us return to Rome, or at least to my short narrative introduction to this chapter. I shall draw this exploration to a close through some reflections on what it might mean that the experience of the numinous is an aesthetic experience. The casual visitor to the Pantheon or St. Peter's might perhaps experience something of the numinous or sacred, and this, I assume, is one of the reasons why so many visit these monuments. If a person experiences something like this, the history of the places as well as

---

67    Fischer-Lichte 2008, p. 204.
68    Gumbrecht 2004, p. 85, see also pp. 16–18.
69    Ricœur 1995, p. 51.

their former and contemporary uses are parts of such an experience and also, and perhaps importantly, of their material form. Visiting the Pantheon or St. Peter's carries the potential of such an experience, not only because of any ideas we might have of them but also for their atmosphere, that multisensory  impression they evoke in us through and because of their appearance. Such impressions are not only visual; all of our senses play a role: the tactile feeling of the Pantheon's concrete, the smell of dust and sometimes of incense that surrounds us, the memory of bread and wine for those of us who go to communion, the acoustics of that vast space and, of course, the sight of the play of light. The Pantheon and St. Peter's are only examples of the loci of such experiences; I have chosen them simply because they are quite well-known to many. Other similar buildings could, *mutatis mutandis*, work in a similar way.

If I am correct in arguing that power and performance are dialectically related in the experience of the sacred, then the experience of the sacred can also be an aesthetic, multisensory  experience. Without the circumscribing edifice in all these aspects that both evoke in us and shield us from the sacred, how much of it would we experience? Modern culture as well as modern Christianity have emphasized the cognitive faculties and also sight as the sense associated with them, and, perhaps as a result, we seem to have forgotten the experience of being an embodied as well as a spatial creature. But that does not mean that the atmospheric qualities of an experience of space have disappeared from everyday life, only that they have become more unarticulated, especially in much academic discourse.[70] To retrieve a sense of that experience through discursive articulation might both make us more aware of it and give us the means of a critical assessment of it. But to retrieve it, we need to be more mindful of its actual, material form. It is not so much that this form only exemplifies sacredness; rather, it participates in that experience through producing it. To articulate such experiences, we need also heed their specific characteristics: even though there might be commonalities between different experiences of the sacred, generated by different edifices, their distinct qualities are as important for rising above (or specifically addressing) mere generalities that might once again obscure the concrete experiences. The phenomenological study of sacred spaces might have something in common with cartography, in that they both attend to the specifics of the aesthetic experiences of these spaces, to their everyday atmospheres.

---

70    On this topic, see, for instance, Böhme 2013, and Gumbrecht 2004.

I noted in my account of my short stroll in Rome in the beginning of this chapter that, even though there are common denominators between the experiences of the Pantheon and of St. Peter's, these sites are both distinct in the way the experience of the sacred is staged in them. In classic literature on the sacred, some of which has been discussed here, the emphasis is on the general rather than the specific and on the abstract and cognitive – the myth, if you will – rather than the concrete and experiential – the form and matter. Although some form of generalization and abstractness is unavoidable in inquiries of this kind, we should not stop there. In a discussion of the atmospheric qualities of experiencing the numinous in and through an edifice, the specifics of that edifice need to enter the discussion. The atmosphere's mode of existence is situated between subject and object, between the visitor to the Pantheon and the building itself, and to avoid giving the impression of that atmosphere as something existing only in the mind of the visitor, the specifics of the building become important for our understanding of its particular atmosphere. What Gumbrecht says about a literary work is also true of a building: "By 'concreteness' I mean that every atmosphere and every mood – as similar as they may be to others – has the singular quality of a material phenomenon".[71] To attend to that "singular quality of a material phenomenon" through discursive accounts of aesthetic experience would, according to Gumbrecht, "reactivate a feeling for the bodily and for the spatial dimensions of our existence".[72] The discursive description needs to attend to the intuitive impression as closely as possible to catch sight of how the numinous manifests itself. To understand the numinous is, of course, of utmost importance, but, in the face of this phenomenon, like so many other aesthetic experiences, we need to be aware of the limits and shortcomings of most descriptions, academic or other. In some rare moments they might perhaps inspire an atmosphere in the reader, as literature often does, but more often they need to rest content with gesturing toward it.[73]

---

71    Gumbrecht 2012, pp. 14–15.
72    Gumbrecht 2004, p. 118.
73    Cf. Gumbrecht 2012, p.16.

# 7.
## Walking in the City

In the last chapter, I went for a short stroll in Rome. Now I would like to take a longer walk and visit three different places in three different cities: first I will enter Paddington Station in London, then walk through the north side of Örgrytevägen and Mässans gata in my hometown Gothenburg and, finally, return for a longer visit to the Pantheon in Rome. These three different places exemplify three different experiences of atmospheres that could be found in some form, I think, in any city, atmospheres that belong together with three distinct kinds of spaces: the gate, the corridor and the temple. If a good portion of this book has been concerned up until now with understanding the concept of atmospheres through specific examples of concrete spaces, the aim of this final chapter is to understand some specific spaces through the concept of atmosphere.

In this way, I hope to fulfil to some extent the call for concreteness in Hans Ulrich Gumbrecht's suggestion, quoted at the end of the last chapter, that "every atmosphere and every mood" corresponds to "the singular quality of a material phenomenon".[1] By undertaking a kind of ethnographic description of these three spaces in their distinct specificity, I aim to describe more comprehensively the way we encounter atmospheres in our everyday lives, how they affect us, how we respond to them and how they configure our relationships to the world and to the existential significance of spatiality in general. An exploration of some of the places and spaces I encounter in London, Gothenburg and Rome may well, precisely in their distinctive "singular quality", illuminate places and spaces elsewhere.

*The Gate: London Paddington*

I walk briskly along the platform. All the other passengers who have disembarked from my train are also purposefully heading to their respective

---

1    Gumbrecht 2012, pp. 14–15.

destinations, so it's important not to take a wrong step or accidentally run over someone with my small suitcase on rather unstable wheels. In the early hours of the morning, the air is chilly; the constant train traffic and the Victorian arched steel and glass roof add a certain rawness to the air here. I get a whiff of dirt but also of coffee from one of the many coffee shops offering refreshments to morning-weary commuters on their way to work or meetings or wherever they're going.

My recurring experience when getting off the shuttle from Heathrow in London Paddington is of space. Paddington is usually my gateway to London when I fly from Landvetter, Gothenburg's airport, on the early morning plane. From the moment the plane lands at Heathrow until I have passed through passport control, bought a ticket from one of the vendors who are ready to let us stressed-out travellers run our errands as quickly as possible and taken the twenty-minute train ride to Paddington, I am still travelling; only when I step off the platform have I arrived. The first of the three kinds of space I want to explore in this final chapter on spatiality in the city, along with the corridor and the temple, is the gateway, and in Paddington I am struck by the open space as capacity or possibility.

This feeling probably has to do with the imposing glazed roof arching over the platforms, which has defined the station since it opened in 1854, originally in the form of three arches broken by two transverse axes of the transept and supplemented by a further arch in 1913–14.[2] The space is punctuated by slender columns that anchor the arches to the platforms. The original roof, like the rest of the station, was designed by the engineer Isambard Kingdom Brunel (1806–1859). Measuring 213 metres by 73 metres, when it was built, it covered the largest train shed in the world. Brunel is considered to be one of the most important British designers of Victorian industrialisation and undoubtedly worked at a time when a number of conditions, economic, political, social and technological, were in place to make his achievements possible.[3] One of the conditions that enabled an industrial revolution in Victorian England was the development of a national infrastructure where steam locomotives could rapidly transport crops, raw materials and manufactured goods, creating a common market for the whole of Britain. Educated in both England and his family's native France, Brunel excelled in many areas of engineering, including tunnels and bridges, but it is probably for his work on the Great Western Railway that he is best remembered. Here he showed himself to be a talented

---

2    See Brindle 2004, especially pp. 101–123 on its architecture.
3    See Brindle 2008, pp. 11–23.

architect in his designs for railway stations, combining technical expertise with good taste and an eye for detail.

An arched glass roof over a metal structure was not unknown at the time. Brunel was inspired by earlier railway stations in England and abroad but especially by the Crystal Palace, built in Hyde Park for the London Exhibition of 1851, a distinctive symbol of industrialism and modernity. The Crystal Palace was designed by Joseph Paxton, but Brunel was deeply involved in the building committee for the exhibition, with weekly meetings with the committee and visits to the building site. The same team that built the Crystal Palace also built Paddington Station but with Brunel as the architect. Though on a much smaller scale than the Crystal Palace, the station's glass and steel structure conveyed dreams that extend beyond (or perhaps, more accurately, alongside) technological advances and what they made possible, a dream in which the transparent boundlessness of the glass evokes an almost weightless feeling in the animated visitor.[4]

The Crystal Palace is a central symbol of modernity, both in terms of its construction and space and its display of the technological achievements of the Industrial Revolution, but it is possible that the railway station is an equally important symbol. The building was moved in 1854 from Hyde Park to what became known as Crystal Palace Park in south London and burned down in 1936, but Paddington, like hundreds of other stations, remains in use. Above all, the everyday use of the railway station is what establishes its primacy as a symbol of modernity. Here, modernity actually took place; it wasn't just exhibited. The railway itself is the fulfilment of modernity's dream of rapid communication, which, with the help of technology, partially or completely removes a human being's attachment to a particular place. Of course, the kind of mobility that is possible in the early twenty-first century could never have been dreamed of in the mid-nineteenth century, but in the two hundred years since the first passenger railway opened in 1825 in England, railroads have been central to the mobility that we now seem to take for granted. Not only did it allow for transporting goods and raw materials, but travelling for people became possible in a completely different way than before. The expansion of the railways for freight transport also meant that they became more accessible for passenger transport and vice versa, and the infrastructure network that connected key nodes of the economy thus also made personal travel possible in a completely new way.

---

4    See Brindle 2004, pp. 31–37 and Giedion 1967, pp. 247–253.

Here the railway station becomes important, not only as a kind of pause or comma in the long and winding sentences of the railway, and not only as a communication node between different sections of the journey. In my own journey from my home in Gothenburg to my destination in London, Heathrow airport is an example of a communication node. Once I land at Heathrow, as I said, I have not "arrived"; airports are generally only a node, as further transport is required to reach the destination. I only "arrive" when I reach Paddington. The railway station is a gateway in a qualified sense, not just an opening between two different spaces but a kind of transition where we enter a new way of being in the world, a threshold. Not surprisingly, the railway station has featured frequently in literature since the 1850s.

For illustrative purposes, we can recall the role played by the railway station in J.K. Rowling's Harry Potter books: King's Cross station, another classic London station from the 1850s, is the terminus of the Hogwarts Express, which runs to platform 9 3⁄4. This is a gateway between the muggle world and the wizard world. For the children going to Hogwarts for their wizarding education, it is here, on this fictional platform, that they change worlds. In earlier children's literature, author Michael Bond in 1958 used Paddington as the place where the bear with the same name as the station entered the human world. Not quite as drastic but also not entirely dissimilar, Paddington is for many a gateway to the city of London: here the traveller enters a global city populated by dreams, opportunities and risks after an often monotonous and uncomfortable journey. Paddington station's peculiar contrast between interior and exterior also reinforces its character as a gateway. Brunel's original plan was for its structure to be more conspicuous externally as well, but it ended up being more interior than exterior: the station is located in a hollow, and its spacious interior is not matched by an imposing exterior. Instead, its exterior becomes the city: London.

The railway station is a transition or gateway between the state of travelling and the state of visiting; only when I step out onto the platform at Paddington have I arrived and am ready to face London and all that I will do there. My experience is spatially embodied by the roof arching over my arrival platform, including its transept. I experience this not only as a physical space but also as the possibilities that lie ahead of me and that I enter as soon as my foot touches the concrete of the platform. The eclectically ornamented wrought iron arched trusses give a vivid first impression of arrival. The physical space that opens outwards through the glass roof corresponds to the existential space of the city's possibilities.

Built as a terminus for the Great Western Railroad, Paddington is in this sense a portal or a lock in which I am moved between different states. Steven Brindle's authoritative work on Paddington describes an "atmosphere of expectation", which fits with my experience.[5]

I sense all this when I finally arrive after travelling too early in the morning. Now the rest of the day opens up in an atmosphere of anticipation. Here I am in a different place from home; here I will do other things, see things that are not part of my everyday life. I leave the station via Praed Street, where the smokers line up, on foot to Marylebone, where I usually have a coffee. But am I the only one experiencing this? When I arrived at Paddington, I didn't really know anything about the engineer Isambard Kingdom Brunel, nothing about how he was inspired by the Crystal Palace, nor did I take the time to study the glass roof and Victorian ornaments at one of the station's entrances. It was more as a sensation or a mood that I experienced in the correspondence between physical and existential space. Everything I know about the history of the railway station and its architect I read afterwards. Perhaps it was more a subjective feeling, an expression of my experience of coming to London again, than anything to do with Paddington railway station as such?

Of course, I carry my memories, my mood and my hopes as I walk through London Paddington. But, as we have seen in previous chapters, relegating our moods to the subjective all too easily overlooks the fact that we as humans are corporeal beings who exist in space as a medium for our lives.[6] The concrete spaces that we inhabit, move in, curiously visit, occupy and pass through are not neutral containers for whatever appears in our minds. Concrete spaces offer and present both opportunities and resistance in our experience of them. If it is true that my subjective mood affects my experience of the room, it is equally true that my experience of changing rooms affects my subjective mood. So, the rooms we enter are crucial to our moods. As a concrete example, London Paddington, with its space and its glass and iron structures, cannot be replaced by a hangar or sports hall without changing the atmosphere. The fact that the station was built at and for the dawn of the Industrial Revolution is not irrelevant; it is in some sense designed to evoke the very mood I have been trying to describe, of forward motion and the play of possibilities but also of a passage through a gateway. If London Paddington had instead been more reminiscent of the Padel Centre at Delsjön in Gothenburg, which is essentially an empty

---

5    Brindle 2004 preface.
6    See Bollnow 2011, pp. 19–25.

hangar with a broken roof and simple sheet metal walls large enough to accommodate a number of padel courts, there would probably not have been a greater sense of modernity and self-reliance. It would not be inaccurate to say that London Paddington as it is now designed actually *wants* something specific for me, a desire that is expressed in the very design of its spaces. Concrete spaces are not neutral but carry meanings.

How do we articulate the idea that concrete spaces want something from us in a way that both corresponds to this experience and avoids personalising the spaces in a way that ascribes to them a kind of human-like agency? If they have an agency, it is a specific spatial agency. One reason for this difficulty is probably the existential reality that we live in space in such an obvious way that we take it for granted, as part of our everyday life, and do not articulate our relationship to it in any particularly elaborate way.[7] Anyone who does not work as an architect, interior designer or urban planner, and therefore has the direct task of imagining the impact of space on people, has probably not practised the nuances, in words nor images, that are required to uncover all the existential dimensions of space. However, my inability to articulate these dimensions does not mean that they do not affect me, just as I do not need to know anything about Brunel's construction of Paddington in order to experience its impact on me. Like many people who work professionally to shape the relationship between human beings and space in concrete terms, I suspect, I must therefore try to interpret my knowledge of an experience that is implicit rather than clearly stated.

Brindle wrote of Paddington's atmosphere of expectation even if he, as far as I can understand, does not relate it to the new phenomenology and its discussion of atmospheres. As we have seen, atmosphere is not something that can be found either in human beings alone or in space alone but, rather, exist *between* human beings and space; it is produced space but also the space of nature. The atmosphere is, so to speak, neither completely self-produced nor completely determined by what is outside humans. It is produced by what is outside humans, for example, in its aesthetic form and properties in the full range of the senses, so that it can influence, perhaps even *will* something with a human being, who thus becomes its co-creator. In the case of the railway station, its aesthetic qualities, its impressions that the organisation of its form makes on human perception, are responsible for how people find themselves in these spaces. The design of a concrete railway station produces an atmosphere that distinguishes the station from other buildings as well as from many other railway stations. It puts people

---

7    Cf. Casey 1997, p. x.

in the spotlight with an invitation to experience themselves and their surroundings in a certain way and therefore also to behave in a certain way. I don't dance along the platform like a ballet dancer but, rather, I fall into the rhythm of my rapid steps and experience how I am now ready, with my own agenda, to join the others on their way into the city. The architecture carries a certain choreography; it is a score for my movements.

The atmosphere we encounter in the room – and even the absence of any perceptible atmosphere is, so to speak, also an atmosphere – is multisensory, even synesthetic, in which the individual sensory perceptions are amplified and merge into each other.[8] Its aesthetic qualities include sight, smell, hearing, touch and, to some extent, taste. Böhme uses the term "acoustic furniture" to refer to the acoustic qualities of a particular room. In some rooms, such acoustic furniture may be deliberate and designed, such as in the shopping centre where blaring music is meant to put us in a relaxed and consumer-friendly mood, but it doesn't have to be deliberate to be acoustic furniture.[9] When Brunel designed London Paddington, we can assume that he did not plan in detail the acoustic furnishings that characterise the station, but nevertheless the squeaking of the train wheels against the rails, the whistles signalling departure and (in our time) the announcement of the next departure by the public address system speak volumes and tell us that we are in a train station. Similarly, there is an olfactory design that appears, in this case, at least as much given by circumstance as consciously planned. I have rudimentarily reproduced this above by mentioning dirt and coffee, but surely we also register steel, concrete, the presence of other people and much more. To reproduce in detail the olfactory sensations of a particular room probably requires a rather highly trained sense of smell that is able to distinguish between different odours so as not to appear as mere fantasy.[10] But in a way this doesn't really matter because in the everyday case the olfactory sensations meet us in an undifferentiated way that still allows us to unmistakably identify the olfactory design of a railway station without having to really concentrate on the task. It is simply part of the way we encounter and absorb the space. The room is furnished for all our senses.

The point of briefly mentioning the acoustic and olfactory design of London Paddington here is to show how it is not the Victorian arched

---

8    See here Pallasmaa 2012.
9    Böhme 2019a, p. 47.
10    In Nordström 1928, p. 188 f. the author indirectly claims to be able to distinguish odours from at least twenty five different sources, which does not seem very credible.

glass roof alone that evokes the mood that meets me when I set foot on London Paddington's platform. It is sight, hearing, smell and probably in an even more subtle way also touch and taste that together, in a synesthetic way, meet me there and put me in the mood of anticipation, morning tiredness and ambition that I register just below the more conscious and intentional layers of my mind. In a sense, then, the atmosphere of London Paddington locates me in physical space, but inseparably from this, and in the same act, I am also located in my own inner space in the form of a mood. London Paddington, by virtue of its atmosphere, is a "gateway" due to its "metaxological" character; its gateway character belongs to the intermediate layer between human beings and spatiality.[11]

I have spoken above about spatiality in terms of agency, that a particular space "wants" something of me, to draw attention to how it is the atmosphere of the room, which is not something purely subjective, that puts us in a certain mood. But at the same time, it is also important to point out that this "will" of the room can, to a certain extent, be derived from the intention of the designer, even if it cannot be reduced to this. Brunel had neither the intention nor the ability to design or master all the acoustic and olfactory aspects of London Paddington, but at the same time he designed the station as a whole with certain aims that were well in line with the industrial revolution and its claims to reshape human existence. Utopians throughout history, from Plato onwards, have consistently presented architectural visions as a way of moulding the future human being into an ideal.[12] While their proposals may seem quite utopian in their belief in how architecture contributes to the creation of peace and prosperity, there is truth in the fact that spaces do affect us fundamentally through their atmosphere, even if this is not as easily instrumentalised as at least some philosophers, such as Charles Fourier, hoped. Even when a particular space achieves a kind of semi-autonomous status as times, surroundings and technical possibilities change, it hardly detaches itself completely from the original intentions unless it becomes a completely different space.

As I have previously argued in this book, the "will" of the room does not mean that it has the ability to *force* us to be in a certain mood. There are several reasons for this that I mention in Chapter 2, but let me repeat some of them here. First, it is possible that we are insensitive to many of the stimuli we encounter: I may be preoccupied with a personal problem that leaves me cold to them, or I may simply lack a sense of smell and taste, which

---

11    See Desmond 1995.
12    See, for example, Luckhurst 2019, pp. 43–69.

means that the impact of the atmosphere is not as strong. Or, in an attempt to be critical, we allow the atmosphere to rise up to the intentional layers of our consciousness to be scrutinised. Perhaps there are good reasons why we are suspicious of the "will" of the space and have decided not to let our mood be swept away by it. However, in an anthropologically fundamental sense, we are always involved in some atmosphere that envelops us, and it is only in relation to this fundamental involvement that it makes sense to speak of a critical approach to it. The person who lives completely outside the atmosphere would be a person who is alienated from fellow human beings and depersonalised.[13]

Thus, although we cannot be neutral or avoid the atmosphere of a space altogether, it does not assume a deterministic relationship towards us. I have repeatedly, and perhaps at odds with some of the philosophers of atmosphere, distinguished between mood, as the realm of us human beings, and atmosphere, as the realm of space.[14] Human beings and space neither merge completely nor constitute two distinct entities but relate to each other metaxologically; they are united in the gap that precedes any division between subject and object or between human beings and space.[15] Therefore, we also have the possibility to relate actively and not merely passively to space; even if its atmosphere does things to us, we also respond to its appeal in different ways, deviating from its "will" to some extent, bigger or smaller, or following or even playing with and transforming it into something else. The fact that the atmosphere of the room is reflected in our perceptions of it and affects our mood should not be understood as meaning that the alternatives are either a passive-sensory relationship to the room or an active-intentional one. Rather, the relationship is performative, where the atmosphere of the space is primary, but where our response combines activity and passivity. It is more like a dance in which the architecture sets the rhythm and tempo.

Each space carries a unique atmospheric stamp. Although London Paddington is probably a fairly typical expression of a railway station of the late industrial revolution in whose womb the railway station as such was conceived, other railway stations are characterised by partly different atmospheres. For several reasons related to atmosphere, I am immediately aware that I am in London Paddington and not in, say, the Central Station in Gothenburg, with its relatively low ceilings and messy layout; Kyoto

---

13    See Fuchs 2018.
14    See further Hasse 2015b, pp. 227–248.
15    For an elaboration on this from a slightly different perspective, see the chapter "Det porösa självet" [The porous self] in Sigurdson 2021b.

Station, with its huge staircase, terraces and 11-storey shopping centre or Stazione Termini in Rome, with its S-curved roof and rather chaotic organisation.[16] While there are obviously family resemblances between railway stations, particularly since the four examples I have mentioned here were all originally built around the same time, variations in architectural vision, redevelopment, urban environment, culture, population and other factors are too great to offer any universal phenomenology of railway station atmosphere. Drawing attention to the atmospheric characteristics of the individual railway station, in this case London Paddington, helps to deepen our atmospheric competence for the station itself and also in relation to other stations, other gates and even other spaces.

### The Corridor: The north side of Örgrytevägen/Mässans gata

Every morning on my way to work or down to the centre of Gothenburg I walk along the northern side of a busy street called Örgrytevägen. Just after crossing the Mölndalsån river on my way west, I come to a place that stretches almost all the way to the end of the street, to a junction called Korsvägen and which is surrounded by a small square just outside the main entrance to the Swedish Exhibition & Congress Centre. I have passed by here thousands of times. Quite often I ask myself if it is not one of the most inhospitable of all the places I regularly pass by or visit. Should the city of Gothenburg not be more interested in one of its main junctions being characterised by a welcoming and hospitable atmosphere, both for residents and tourists? Above all, this path is an example of a kind of space that is not uncommon in the contemporary city and therefore interesting in itself.

Back to my walking route: just before I reach Mölndalsån on my way west, I pass Liseberg station, a commuter train station where trains between Gothenburg and Kungsbacka and Gothenburg and Borås stop. Thus, the pedestrian is met here by a number of people who commute to or from the centre of Gothenburg and disembark or embark station. Many tourists also come here on their way to the nearby Liseberg amusement park. After the station and just before the Mölndalsån, I pass Focushuset on my right. This is a six-storey, 50,000-square-metre office building, car park and shopping centre that houses one of Gothenburg's largest ICA stores and also a large shop for wine and alcohol. Beyond the Mölndalsån,

---

16   For brief descriptions of a large number of railway stations, see Bakerson 2010.

on the two-lane south side of Örgrytevägen, which is separated from the similarly two-lane north side by a double-track tram line, is the amusement park, operated by the city of Gothenburg since 1923. Liseberg is the largest amusement park in the Nordic region and has regularly been Sweden's most popular destination in recent years. Its main entrance is located here. The Gothenburg City Council has decided on a major expansion of Liseberg to the south, with an "experience centre" and an adventure pool. These plans are central to Gothenburg's 400th anniversary, originally planned for 2021 but postponed to 2023 due to the coronavirus pandemic. In 2024, just before its opening, the building that housed the adventure pool burned down due to an accident.

If we stay on the north side of Örgrytevägen, we walk past the side of the Swedish Exhibition & Congress Centre, where the entrance and exit to the 41,000 square meters of exhibition space is located. This is a building with large picture windows above a foundation of the yellow brick typical of Gothenburg. Then we meet the three towers that make up Hotel Gothia Towers, a four-star hotel with a five-star section, built in a rather contemporary style from the 1980s, with a third tower that was completed in 2015. A fourth tower is planned for the future, but Hotel Gothia Towers already has 1,200 rooms. It also hosts a number of restaurants, including the Michelin-starred Upper House Dining and the popular Heaven 23, which in 2006 sold more than 100,000 of its signature dish, the prawn sandwich, and also offers a panoramic view of the city. In other words, the little passage that is the focus of my interest here is surrounded by places that very much define the commercial life of Gothenburg, particularly in terms of tourism. Around the corner to the right on a street called Skånegatan, when I follow Örgrytevägen all the way to Korsvägen, a lot of Gothenburg's signature sites are lined up: an amusement park, a conference centre, a multi-sports stadium, a multi-screen cinema, and eventually a football stadium (Nya Ullevi). If you turn left instead, south on the street Södra vägen, you will find both Universeum, a national science centre, and the Museum of World Culture on the eastern side. Örgrytevägen, Södra vägen and Skånegatan are linked by one of Gothenburg's most important public transport hubs that I have already repeatedly mentioned, Korsvägen, which will be even more important after the completion of the West Link as a new commuter train station. The city of Gothenburg's website states that "Korsvägen is a place where everyday life meets culture, events and business",[17] officially highlighting this area as

---

17   https://goteborg.se/wps/portal/start/byggande--lantmateri-och-planarbete/
     kommunens-planarbete/plan--och-byggprojekt/!ud/p/z1/hY9Ba4NAFIR_

central to the city. One can therefore assume that the city of Gothenburg is doing everything it can to make the area as attractive as possible for those who move around in it. Even passages like the one that is the focus of my interest here naturally contribute to the overall impression; thus, it is surprising how inhospitable it appears. However, I am not primarily interested in the reason why it is the way it is but what kind of place it is and why it conveys such an inhospitable atmosphere.

I think it is correct to characterise the passage along Mölndalnsån to Korsvägen on the north side of Örgrytevägen as an urban corridor. The word "corridor" comes from the Italian verb *currere* meaning to run, which seems well chosen for this particular passage. Corridors come in many forms, but British literary scholar Peter Luckhurst, in an extensive study of the cultural history of the corridor, has shown how it is a typically modern space.[18] In modern history, the corridor has stood for both utopia and dystopia, but the urban corridor in question is in some ways too insignificant, too boring, to even claim to be particularly dystopian. It belongs to the kinds of corridors in the city that are only meant to be passed through and do not claim to be places themselves. Of course, even such corridors have their own particular atmospheres, and an urban corridor in an area such as this, with its cultural and economic importance to Gothenburg, *could* be designed to encourage the feeling of going somewhere and thus instil a certain expectation in passers-by. But not even the feeling of eventually arriving at something colours the corridor here.

Is this a kind of ideal corridor, a place that is a material realisation of the very idea of the corridor as a passage? Not really. Those who pass through here on their way to work or to some leisure activity usually encounter a number of obstacles in the form of lorries that are waiting to drop off or pick up goods at the Swedish Exhibition Centre, taxis on their way to the hotel, competition between pedestrians and cyclists moving in both directions or lawn mowing on the small slope that faces Örgrytevägen and separates it from the Mässans gata. When the wind is blowing, it is difficult to move as a pedestrian in this exposed passage. The perception of the passage's surface up to the hotel driveway – when trucks are not parked on the way in – is of

---

Sw9e973VZd-mt7WQEFeSlAaiewmm2Rjb6MpqK_TX1x4LLZnbMN_
ADFgowHbVZ1NXY-O76jb70srjjmfPKuUat6vFEtd7s1tuTL5FI-
BwD7BzjP9II5Rzn44iXiHPBDdKpoQ6N0-JNCRNTvACFmwf_Jt7H5szlOkG
ZaIi5BwysM2pZdNry5AlFEsSnMSCSMmYfqbr7pSoGmxwFxdcYB9hfnQdx3
54jDDCaZpY7X19c2xwEf7VuPphhOIXCH1bfO0v7UEN-uEbtRxrJQ!!/dz/d5/
L2dBISEvZ0FBIS9nQSEh/. Access 201104.
18    Luckhurst 2019.

an empty space that cannot be used for anything, facing a side facade with gates and doors of a purely functional nature and a rather arbitrarily placed digital screen projecting advertising for the city's events. The feeling is of passing through the backside of the event route, through a leftover space. The kind of corridor in question here is akin to what Luckhurst refers to as the monotonous and uniform corridor of bureaucracy, but with the proviso that the monotony here is not derived from a consciously planned uniformity but, rather, an absence of any particular intention other than that of passage.[19] It is not possible, for the reasons I have mentioned, to speak of a *functional* passage for traffic where all aesthetic/atmospheric considerations have given way since it is hardly optimal for pedestrians, cyclists or motorists; if we widen the perspective to the fact that it is also part of the street with some of Gothenburg's signature sites, it is even less functional since it hardly instils a welcoming and expectant feeling in the visitor. It constitutes a remnant between the more significant spaces that define the Mässans gata.

Here it is probably reasonable to pose a counter-question to the above description: what should one really expect from a corridor of this kind? In some sense, after all, the tangential corridor is functional in nature and therefore has no inherent inclination or need to become a genuine place. No one is claiming that the corridor is a place that can be inhabited. To describe the atmospheric significance of the kind of corridor I am discussing here, we can draw on French anthropologist Marc Augé's distinction between a place and a non-place.[20] If the place is characterised by being relational, historical and identity-creating, the non-place is characterised by the opposite. Being a historical place means, first of all, integrating the previous places that have been on the same site, even if they are relegated to the background. The non-place, on the other hand, relegates the previous places to memory, a memory that is not embodied in buildings and urban planning as such but where these do not create any relationship to the past at all.[21] Nor do the non-places have an identity of their own but are found in recognisable condition all over the world: means of transport, airports, hotel chains, playgrounds and supermarkets, for example. They have no "here" of their own, so to speak. Or you could say that these spaces, despite being used by people, are rarely or never transformed into places.[22]

---

19 Luckhurst 2019, p. 15.
20 See Augé 1995, pp. 75–115.
21 Cf. Assmann 2007.
22 Cf. Certeau 1984, pp. 117–118, an argument that also underpins Augé.

Finally, and perhaps most interesting here, non-places are also non-relational, meaning that those who stay or pass through them do not create any kind of relationship with them. They remain non-symbolised in that they are not part of any kind of meaning-making network of symbolic activities. For a place to become a place, it must be made so by the actions of people, which means that those for whom a place is a place establish some kind of relationship with it. According to Yi-Fu Tuan, we turn a space into a place by making use of it, but in this case of the urban corridor, the use does not stick.[23] However, the non-place is not just a space to which no relationship has yet been established, a potential place; it is a space already realised as a non-place in contradistinction to a place. The northern part of Örgrytevägen is not a place and does not seem to be able to become one. The non-place is a limit concept, so no space must fully realise the relationality of the non-place in order to bear its features. Significant events can happen anywhere, even in the most anonymous or inhospitable environments. But although some significant events have taken place along Örgrytevägen, such as on September 30, 2017, when the road was blocked for a few hours by police and demonstrators from the Nazi Nordiska motståndsrörelsen, and on November 15–17, 2017, when it was completely closed off for an EU summit, none of these events have left any trace, neither tangible nor symbolic. The importance of the space is created only by the signs regulating traffic and the seemingly arbitrary placement of advertising screens. The only human measure that seems applicable to this part of Örgrytevägen is how long it takes to pass through it. Certainly, it is intertwined with spaces that we can call places, to which people have relationships, but here it is a residual product of those places, and that also characterises its atmosphere. This corridor is a nowhere.

As we have seen in Chapter 3, what the non-place lacks is what Hartmut Rosa calls "resonance". Resonance is encountered where it is possible to appropriate a space in some sense, though not necessarily as a possession.[24] Resonance is a phenomenon that occurs *between* us human beings and our built (and other) environment, like the atmosphere, and it occurs in this sense when something has meaning for us, concerns us in some way and also gives some kind of response; it "wants" something from us, at least by lending itself to us to some extent. If a space is impossible to appropriate, it remains mute, thus effectively impossible to relate to in any way that is perceived as meaningful. Thus, if the corridor is a non-place, it is because

---

23    Tuan 1977, pp. 73, 136–148, 161–178.
24    Rosa 2020, especially pp. 263–265, 281–298, 635–644.

of its lack of resonance potential for the passer-by who, in turn, remains a stranger to and in the space in question. The space does not provide a response that makes the person part of it in any way and makes him or her oscillate, physically, emotionally or cognitively, in response to the space's response. Despite all the pedestrians who move daily along the corridor I have described, they fail to transform this corridor constructed by the urban planners into a genuine place, either through their footsteps or through a narrative of some significant event, and this is both a result of the absence of resonance and the inability to establish it. Here, resonance is more a property of a relationship than an emotional state, in this case between the pedestrian (or any of the other road users) and the corridor.

"In some way" is an important qualification of how we engage with a space, how we make it a place: the ideal is not that every place should feel like home. There are places that do not possess the qualities that characterise a home and that concern us and speak to us in different ways than the home does.[25] Both the gateway that I have already discussed above in the form of London Paddington and the temple that I discussed in the previous chapter and that I will soon return to in the form of the Pantheon in Rome are definitely places without taking on the character of a home at all. Nor does a space need to evoke strong feelings of participation to be said to have resonance potential. Here we can probably imagine a scale from lower to higher potential for resonance as an effect of the individual intersection of personal experience, cultural significance and architectural design. But the resonance-less corridor results in an atmosphere of relatively strong alienation or inhospitability, as I have previously called it, where the individual is urged by the physical environment itself to hurry away. According to Thomas Fuchs, the basic experience of being alive is to be in a communicative relationship with the world, and so if the corridor is not in a communicative relationship with the world, it simply does not respond to this basic experience.[26] One travels through it as a living dead. The resonance-free corridor constitutes a specific atmospheric mode of our relationship to the world in which this relationship appears mute and in which we therefore, in a sense, give a negative response (which is in fact an absence of response) by deafening ourselves to it.

Although resonance, according to Rosa, is both an analytical and a normative concept, my use of the term here is primarily analytical.[27] There

---

25    Rosa 2020, pp. 602–610.
26    Fuchs 2018, pp. 119, 173–174.
27    Rosa 2020, p. 293 et seq.

is certainly a legitimate normative critique of human alienation in our time in Rosa's use of the term, but my use of the term here is about trying to capture an experience of space rather than commenting on a small part of Gothenburg's urban planning. The muteness that characterises the corridor that stretches along northern Örgrytevägen and is surrounded by the short street called Mässans gata is hardly an effect of a particular architectural style but can probably be found in all architectural styles, from classicist to modernist. Architects are well aware of these spaces, as interstitial spaces or SLOAP (spaces left over after planning). Insight into the atmospheric mode that characterises the not-so-resonant corridor is important to consider, as it articulates a way of experiencing space that could contribute to experiences of alienation in urban space. It is one thing that the inhospitable passage that I have dwelt on here hardly seems appropriate given the great importance of these streets for Gothenburg, even if it is not a big deal that it is boring to pass through on the way to work – after all it is only a few minutes' walk. Perhaps it is also inevitable that cities contain some such inhospitable by-products in the form of corridors, as all spaces can hardly be experienced as resonant and inviting in the same way. Perhaps it is not even ideal for everything in the city to be involved in the aestheticisation of urban space that has taken place in many European metropolises since the 1990s and which often becomes a form of compensation for the general indifference of the city.[28] In this case, boredom as a human mood corresponds to inhospitality as the atmosphere of the space. In any case, resonance is something that cannot be entirely planned because it contains an element of uncontrollability.[29] However, what is sometimes missing in critical discussions of urban space and architecture is a vocabulary that helps us to articulate experiences of space in a more precise and complex way and to avoid simplistically explaining alienation as an effect of a particular style, such as brutalism or modernism. Here it is important to be able to articulate these less appealing atmospheres, too.


*The Temple: Pantheon, Rome*


Returning to the Pantheon one more time, I arrive at Piazza della Rotonda via one of the small streets from the east, Via dei Pastini, or from the north-east, Via degli Orfani. Along these streets, as almost everywhere

---

28    See Hasse 2015b, pp. 174–201.
29    See Rosa 2020, p. 295 and 2020b.

in this part of Rome's historic centre known as the Campo Marzio or Field of Mars, the visitor is greeted by a veritable witch's cauldron of tourists, shops, bars, restaurants (some very good) and mopeds. When I arrive at Piazza della Rotonda whether on the move or having stopped to look at it, I am always struck by the massive weight with which the Pantheon seems to be anchored to the ground. In the midst of these medieval streets with their fairly intense crowds, I am greeted by this monumental temple. The Pantheon consists, as previously mentioned, of a portico with three rows of a total of sixteen granite columns with Corinthian capitals under a pediment that leads via a vestibule to the forty-three-metre-high brick rotunda covered by a concrete dome with an *oculus* at its centre. The Pantheon is one of Rome's most famous landmarks and has been widely copied by architects around the world in churches but also town halls, museums, libraries and universities.[30] I like the hustle and bustle of this part of Rome; the Eternal City has always been a tourist city, drawing people from all over the world, from its time as the centre of the Roman Empire to its position as the centre of Christianity, including an entertainment scene long associated with the Campo Marzio itself.[31] Arguably, Rome has always been rather messy, despite attempts to bring order to the urban space.[32] In other words, there is no reason to believe that Rome is any less authentic now than it was, even if it began its transformation into a modern tourist city at the end of the twentieth century. In this hustle and bustle, the Pantheon sits like a granite and concrete exclamation point at the centre of a lively conversation.

The history of the Pantheon is well known: construction was probably started by the Roman Emperor Trajan (53–117 CE) with the architect Apollodorus, but the temple was completed by the Emperor Hadrian (76–138 CE), perhaps no later than around 126 CE.[33] The pediment's inscription "M-AGRIPPA-L- F-COS-TERTIUM-FECIT'" ["Marcus Agrippa, son of Lucius, Consul for the third time, had this built"] marks the continuity with an earlier temple on the site that burned down in 110 CE, the Consul Marcus Agrippa (63–12 BCE) and early Rome. The Pantheon joins the triangle of the pediment with the square of the vestibule and the circle of

---

30 An interesting connection to modernist sacred architecture is through concrete; see Samuel and Linder-Gaillard 2020.
31 Cf. Reinhardt 2014; Maier 2020.
32 See e.g. Giedion 1967, pp. 75–106.
33 Much of the specific information on the Pantheon is taken from Nordholm 2017, especially pp. 53–60, as well as MacDonald 1976 and Marder and Jones 2015. See also Jenkyns 2013, pp. 351–364.

the temple building itself in a way that seems to follow classical ideals of how the proportions of the temple should relate to each other like the body parts of a well-built human being.[34]

The Pantheon is thus a building that allows us to experience contrasts: between the bustling and flowing urban life of the Campo Marzio and the massive stillness and weight of the building; between the austere granite and emphasis of the outer shell and the inner space of the temple; and, last but not least, in the play between darkness and light in its interior thanks to the vertical light source, the *oculus* or eye, at the top of the dome's centre, with a diameter of about nine meters. This is the only light source in the Pantheon dome, and it is always open. The light beam from the dome's *oculus* reaches the floor once a year, at Midsummer. As we enter the space between the columns of the Pantheon via the vestibule, our horizontal movement stops and is replaced by a vertical movement as our attention is drawn upwards in line with the central axis of the building. The centre of gravity of the relationship between a human being and space shifts from us to the temple as our own activity is replaced by a more passive reception of the light flooding in from above. All these contrasts serve to underpin this experience of a shift in centre of gravity. One moment our gaze takes in the Pantheon as one of Rome's landmarks looming before us, but soon we enter, and now we are the object of the eye's gaze. But while contrasts are what both capture and produce our experience, we must be careful not to perceive them only in terms of binary oppositions. In fact, it is part of the atmosphere of the Pantheon to also hold together the contrasts between outer and inner, active and passive, horizontal and vertical. The verticality of the experience of the Pantheon is not at the expense of its horizontality; it is the same monumental building of granite, brick and concrete that is seemingly eternally anchored in the Piazza della Rotonda that also allows us to experience space, ascent and weightlessness; our celestial flights are still firmly anchored in the earthly. There is no contradiction between them.

The Pantheon is a *temple* (from the Latin *templum*) in the sense of a shrine, a place of worship and adoration of the divine. The word Pantheon is, as mentioned in the previous chapter, a compound of the Greek *pan,* meaning "all", and *theion,* meaning "gods", and literally means "for all the gods". It is unclear whether the building was actually originally called the Pantheon or whether it eventually came to be called that, but during its time as a Roman sanctuary the epithet was certainly apt. It has also been used as a memorial to great men: the artists Raphael and Annibale

---

34    See Vitruvius 1955, book III, chapter 1.

Carracci are buried here, as are the Italian kings Emanuel II and Umberto I. In the early sixth century, after receiving the Pantheon as a gift from the Byzantine emperor Fokas, it was consecrated by Pope Boniface IV as a Christian church under the name of Santa Maria ad Martyres, and thus it is also sometimes referred to as the Santa Maria Rotonda. Even today, the Pantheon is still actively used as a church during certain holidays, even though it is state property. According to an article published on the CNN website, it is the oldest building in the world still in use.[35] Perhaps the Pantheon still deserves its name: the fact that it is a consecrated church and used as such does not deter its ecumenical character as a symbol of human eternal longing and encounter with the numinous.

Although both its exterior and interior have been affected by its changing religious affiliations over time, the basic structure of the Pantheon has remained intact. Pope Urban VIII Barberini (1623–1644) replaced the portico's bronze roof with wooden beams because he needed bronze for cannons. In addition, with the help of architects Carlo Maderno and Francesco Borromini, he also built two towers on the portico that were removed in the 1880s. That these not only look unattractive – one can see them in images from that time – from the point of view of some of the aesthetic ideals of our time but also from the point of view of earlier ideals is clearly shown by the epithet given to them: donkey's ears. Nevertheless, through the ages and across religious boundaries, we can probably assume that the Pantheon has instilled an experience of the sacred in its visitors. The atmosphere we encounter here is a significant expression of an experience of sacredness.

What is meant by sacredness here? An initial definition of the concept can be based on the experience of the numinous, or, in slightly more colloquial terms, the contemplation and grasping of something else that is not within our sphere of control.[36] We need not concern ourselves here with the nature of this other, only note that the experience of the sacred involves an encounter with something that sets a boundary with ourselves and also overwhelms the self. Above I have described the entry into the Pantheon as a slowing down of our own horizontal movement, which is thus replaced by the vertical direction of the gaze. There is an architecturally induced change of movement and mood in which the centre of gravity of the agency of the encounter is shifted from human being to space; it is no longer our eyes but the *oculus* of the dome that is the primary agent in the viewing

---

35    Palumbo 2020.
36    See Otto 1958. For an overview, see Dahl 2010.

process. Thus, if the atmosphere is particularly intense, there is a sense of being watched, as if the *oculus* of the dome were the actual eye of God. Of course, the experience of entering the Pantheon can be very different not only because of the individual's mood but also because of their religious biography. We do not have to assume that the self-conscious Christian who enters the Pantheon as a Christian church experiences exactly the same thing as the more ambivalent tourist who happens to come across the Pantheon in their wanderings in Rome. However, the fact that the Pantheon has functioned both as a Christian church and previously as a Roman temple without changing its basic form suggests that there are experiences of sacredness that transcend denominational boundaries. The ancient Roman who entered the temple to meet the gods and the later Christian or the religiously ambivalent tourist can all probably be assumed to sense something of the sacred; the sacred is the atmosphere we encounter in the Pantheon, and as such it belongs neither to the human mind alone nor, in an absolute sense, to the space, but between them.

For Mircea Eliade, the notion of sacred space was, as we saw in the previous chapter, central to his (quasi-)phenomenology of religion.[37] Here, there is reason to return to his contention that the experience of sacred space involves a break with an understanding of space as homogeneous and neutral. The sacred space is instead heterogeneous, existentially significant and thus also provides a fixed point from which people can orient themselves. The neutral space is instead the purely geometric space, and to the extent that all people orient themselves on the basis of something that they hold to be self-evidently valuable, there are not people who only live in a purely profane space.[38] All spaces that humans perceive are in some way filled with meanings and values. The corridor I have discussed above could possibly be an example of such a profane space, as it does not seem to be devoted to human life at all, but at the same time it might rather be a reminder of the heterogeneity of space thanks to its contrast with a more living space, be it a home, a gate or a temple. In the discussion here, profane space would correspond to Augé's non-place, while sacred space would be a particularly intense experience of place. Eliade mentions the hometown, the place of first love or places in other cities visited in youth as examples of "sacred places", those that have a special significance

---

37   Eliade 1959, especially pp. 20–65.
38   On the ubiquity of the sacred even in the modern world, see Joas, 2017. On why the modern world is not de-enchanted but rather re-enchanted, see Lauter 2014 respectively McCarraher 2019.

or intensity in one's private universe.[39] Experiences of the sacred are not reserved for people with an active and informed relationship with the divine.

Furthermore, the sacred space is characterised by a gateway or threshold that serves as a portal between the everyday and the sacred space. In the case of the Pantheon, I have spoken of the rows of columns and the vestibule as such a threshold, but in a sense one could say that the Pantheon itself is the threshold. The very point of the threshold is that it is a transition, a gateway.[40] Though London Paddington may not be a candidate for the epithet of sacred space, we can note that there is, in fact, a similar threshold function here, namely in the function of being a transition between two qualitatively different spaces: the space of the journey and the space of the city, where the purpose of the station becomes to "attune" the traveller to becoming a visitor. In the case of Paddington, it is primarily a horizontal transition and not, as with the Pantheon and the more traditional sacred space, a vertical one. Or, if the difference between the horizontal and the vertical seems too contrastive, it is a difference in the kind of subjectivity that the atmosphere gives rise to, a more autonomous one based on an atmosphere of expectation or a more porous one based on an atmosphere of contemplation and apprehension. Train stations like Paddington have indeed been called Victorian-era cathedrals, and in some cases they were also inspired by the Pantheon's dome. However, there is still a difference in that the atmosphere of the place "wanting" me to do something is more evident in temples like the Pantheon.[41] The sacred space is simultaneously more intrusive and more secretive; it does not lend itself as easily to being an environment for our own purposes.

The function of the threshold in the temple is both to separate and to hold together; it is a break in the continuity between different spaces that holds them together as discontinuous. In the Pantheon we less obviously cross a threshold than when we pass through Paddington. In the temple we become aware that we are taking a decisive step in a way that does not happen as strongly in the station; in the latter I am not struck by apprehension as I walk out along Praed Street but rather anticipation. Once over the threshold of the temple, it is as if I am struck by something that brings about the aforementioned shift in perspective from observer to observed. Something claims me and demands my contemplation, and this Eliade

---

39   Eliade 1959, pp. 23–24.
40   On thresholds, see, once again, my forthcoming book Sigurdson 2024.
41   DeLaine 1999, p. 150–151.

     

calls a "hierophany", a beholding or manifestation of the sacred. Again, the Pantheon serves as an excellent illustration of this, with its *oculus* watching the visitor from above. However, it is not only the "eye" in the centre of the dome that makes the Pantheon a sacred space but also the construction itself, which in many ways becomes a form of cosmic symbolism: the floor as the earth, the walls as the human world and the dome as the celestial vault that encloses both; the triangle of the pediment, the square of the vestibule and the circular shape of the temple. The Pantheon is a space that accommodates both the ordered and the intangible, placing us in a world that is both our own and unfamiliar.[42]

But can the Pantheon or any other temple really convey an experience of something other? After all, we know that it was Emperor Hadrian who completed the Pantheon, albeit not with his own hands. If this and all the other temples are built by human hands as much as Paddington is, or, for that matter, the north side of Örgrytevägen is, is there any reason to imagine that the experience of sacredness is an encounter with anything else than our own selves? A suggested answer from the previous chapter is that sacred spaces not only produce this experience of numinosity but also manifest it. Although, of course, they are constructed to produce experiences of sacredness – the *oculus* of the dome is not there by accident, so to speak – and this atmospheric potentiality is reinforced by their use as sacred spaces even after they are built, the experience of sacredness is not secondary to human subjectivity but stems from the anthropologically fundamental experience of resonance, of the world not being mute, and of the intangibility I mentioned earlier. The primary world of human experience is not an alienated, neutral non-place but a world where we expect some kind of resonance in order to live. And in this resonance, as its precondition, lies a kind of primal trust in the world as something genuinely other, not just as a projection surface for my subjective fantasies.[43] The experiential heterogeneity of space in general is anthropologically given.[44] In concrete terms, this manifestation rarely occurs alongside any human production; after all, we are all born into a human context. The mistake is probably to see manifestation and production as competing with each other; the fact that production is a response to manifestation does not necessarily mean that they must be temporally separated, just as there is no contradiction between our celestial flights in the Pantheon and its earthly anchorage, or

---

42    Cf. MacDonald 1976, p. 132, which, however, sees the sacred and the secular too
      much as opposites, but especially Jenkyns 2013, p. 364.
43    See Sigurdson 2020, pp. 144–151.
44    See Bollnow 2011, pp. 133–141.

between verticality and horizontality. The fact that the Pantheon is built by human hands does not contradict the fact that the art of building could also manifest something else, as a repetition of numinosity rather than a pure production of it. In fact, the very concept of atmosphere assumes that not everything that is important to us can be reduced to ourselves.

## On Existential Spaces

In his endeavour to distinguish between profane space and sacred space, Eliade contrasts these spaces as homogeneous and heterogeneous respectively. The latter space contains "interruptions", and this heterogeneity is the crucial difference between the sacred and everything else.[45] In other words, he sees a single, decisive rift in space. In the background of Eliade's 1957 argument, we find an experience of the "disenchantment" or "desacralization" of the world that Eliade shared with many of his contemporaries; "disenchantment" or *Entzauberung* is a term coined by Max Weber that has since come to stand for a loss of all transcendent experiences in the modern world, the experiences of being gripped by something beyond the self.[46] If all such experiences disappear, then space itself is transformed into a homogeneous space, one that is not really capable of responding to our attempts to inhabit it in any way. It becomes a space without response, without resonance, a space where we do not and could never belong. In the above discussion of three different spaces, the homogeneous space would above all be reminiscent of the corridor, not necessarily just the northern part of Örgrytevägen but, rather, all the anonymous and seemingly endless corridors of the world that give us a sense of boredom, powerlessness and alienation. It is not surprising that the corridor appears in contemporary horror fiction as a dystopia, a symbol of alienation and the haunted passage where the ghosts of the dead and their history will never rest or reach a gate.[47]

Does Eliade's observation about the homogenisation of space really correspond fully to contemporary experience? The thesis of the disenchantment of the world can be doubted for several reasons: first, the process of modernisation in our time appears much less homogeneous, and its relationship to the sacred, more ambivalent, with hardly any

---

45    Eliade 1959, p. 20.
46    See Joas 2017, pp. 355–417.
47    See Luckhurst 2019; Dahlberg 2009; Davies 2007.

linear desacralisation taking place; second, experiences of transcendence have not disappeared, even if they are more anonymous and not always recognized for what they are. As far as spatiality is concerned, even today it is both possible and quite common to experience and imagine other spaces or heterotopias rather than just neutral, reified space. My discussion of the gate, the corridor and the temple in this chapter is an attempt to show how the experience of space in our time is an experience of spaces that are not at all homogeneous. Maurice Merleau-Ponty as well as other phenomenologists distinguish between geometric space and existential space, arguing that for us as spatial beings, existential space precedes geometric space. Our primary relationship to spatiality is not to be passively in a space as in a container but to actively or mediopassively appropriate it by living in it, discovering it and inhabiting it.[48] This is very much a bodily relationship that precedes our reflection on space. Geometric space is by definition neutral and homogeneous, while existential space exhibits all kinds of interruptions. It does not coincide with geometric space and, thus, is not at all homogeneous but exhibits qualitatively different spatialities that have existential meaning for its inhabitants, both as obstacles and as opportunities.[49] Talking about urban space in an existentially relevant way is therefore about establishing a relationship between the geometric and the existential, between the measurable dimensions of space and the lifeworld, as space is never "affect neutral".[50]

Disenchantment in relation to spatiality is an experience that instead denotes the attempt to reduce the existential space to the geometric, as if the existential space were merely a subjective projection on the objectively given geometric space, thus relegating the atmosphere of the space entirely to the subjective mood of the individual. We can compare this to Schmitz's critique of the "psychological-reductionist-introjectionist" reification of the world, where emotions are supposedly internal to our psyche in a dualistic division between subject and object. That measurable geometric space matters to us humans is self-evident: if I'm walking home, it matters a lot whether it's two kilometres home or twenty; more interestingly, perhaps, the experience of space is not unrelated to the height of the ceiling, the colours and materials of the room and so on. But that geometric space precedes existential space and is the only objective space is less obvious. The process of modernisation that is said to lead to disenchantment is also,

---

48    Merleau-Ponty 1992, p. 258; see also Sigurdson 2022, pp. 94–110.
49    See Bollnow 2011, pp. 17–25.
50    See Hasse 2015b, pp. 120–141.

as Henri Lefebvre has shown, a process in which the reification of space conceals how it is produced and what social relationships encompass it as well as its history and meaning. Instead, the relationship between human beings and space is presented as a utilitarian neutrality, as a mere mute relationship between things.[51] The experience of space *as* homogeneous serves to conceal the social power relations that characterise it by turning it into a seemingly neutral container, a "semantic void" where past (and contemporary) meanings are obliterated.[52] This does not mean that space *is* truly homogeneous, only that there is an interest in representing it *as* such. Thus, the homogenisation of space that Eliade implicitly criticises is not only, and perhaps not even primarily, about the flight of the sacred from an increasingly de-enchanted world with the rise of the natural sciences; it is about the rise of capitalism and its tendency to allow, in the words of Marx and Engels, "everything sacred to be profaned" for economic reasons. The existential space – as Lefebvre and others critically remind phenomenology – is always a political and social space where heterogeneous interruptions are also conditioned by economic, cultural and social class.

In a way, Eliade may be right when he speaks of contemporary space as a homogeneous space, but if so, this is not only because the sacred has been displaced from space but because existential and social heterogeneity as such has been dispossessed, at least in our talk about space when it has been reduced to an existentially neutral discourse. This also means that sacred space relates to existential spatiality in a different way than Eliade intended. Of course, it can still be argued that the sacred space is opposed to the profane if the profane is equated with a space emptied of meaning and memory by turning it into a container or a corridor. But in relation to other existential and political concerns, sacred space is more an aspect of these dimensions of space, a strong value or desire for the other. What the homogeneous, geometric space lacks is a depth that is not apparent at first glance. We cannot know geometric space because it can never be anything other than completely transparent; it is mute because it does not respond to human appeals or want anything from us. Against this homogeneous space there is an alienation that is not merely economic or political. Alienation is also an existential symptom of a lack of resonance.[53] In homogeneous space, people experience an indifferent or even hostile

---

51  Lefebvre 1991; cf. Landzelius 2009.
52  Lefebvre 1991, p. 307.
53  See Rosa 2020, pp. 299–316.

relationship between themselves and the space; if the space is a non-place, alienation is a relationship of non-relationship with that space.

The existential space, on the other hand, corresponds, as Merleau- Ponty says of objects, to the incompleteness of our sensory impressions: beyond every space seen, touched or heard, there is something that eludes my sensations of it even when I try to elicit its meaning.[54] We uncover these meanings of spaces not primarily by studying them as passive objects of our supposedly neutral gaze, touch or hearing but through an act, the act of inhabiting them with others, or, to use the term from Chapters 4 and 5, an act of *oikeiosis* or "inhabiting" that not only experiences the space but first and foremost *lives* the space.[55] Making ourselves at home in spaces does not mean reducing them to something too familiar; those familiar spaces that do not also in some aspect escape our habitation risk losing their resonance, their atmosphere and the desire they embody. In spaces we encounter not only economics and architecture, not only urban planning and urbanisation, but also in and through these dreams, longings, fantasies and hopes. The spaces of the city are not one or the other but both sides constantly intertwined in each other.

The point of phenomenology, a point that I think comes across in its discussion of atmospheres, is that it recognises and reflects on the fact that we live and experience our world in the first person. We are surrounded by atmospheres and relate productively to them in the same way that we breathe in and breathe out. Now that I have finished the book on this topic, I am starting to notice again the atmospheres around me. Atmospheres, in this sense, are neither physical nor mental but indivisible experiences of space and affect. Or, as Finnish architect Juhani Pallasmaa comments, "I dwell in the city and the city dwells in me."[56]

---

54    Merleau-Ponty 1992, p. 214. See Cornell 1997.
55    See Fuchs 2018, p. 311, including note 4.
56    Pallasmaa 2012, p. 43.

Several people have been helpful in large and small ways with this manuscript in its various versions, often without knowing it: Michael Azar, Björn Billing, Claes Caldenby, Espen Dahl, Göran Dahlberg, Jonas Eek, Dag Granath, Tonino Griffero, Klas Grinell, Sepp Gumbrecht, Irina Hron, Maria Johansen, Per Magnus Johansson, Simone Kotva, Johan Kärnfelt, Håkan Möller, Jayne Svenungsson, Fredrik Söderberg, Martin Westerholm, Johan Örn. Mikael Andersson deserves special thanks, not only for asking me to write several of the texts included here, but also because the question solved an orchestration problem in my larger project on existence and spatiality. The work on this project has also been supported by the Swedish National Heritage Board. Many thanks.

The first five chapters have been published in Swedish as *Atmosfärer: En introduktion* (Stockholm/Umeå: Andersson Örn, 2023); Chapter 6 as "Numinous Edifices: Aesthetic Experiences of Sacred Spaces", *Svensk teologisk kvartalskrift*, 99 (2023), pp. 49–72; and the final chapter in Swedish as "Porten, korridoren, templet: Om rum i staden", *Arche: Tidskrift för psykoanalys, humaniora och arkitektur*, no 88–89 (2024). They have all been edited for this book. I appreciate the opportunity to have them published in this format as well.

This book marks a threshold in my professional life. The Department of Literature, History of Ideas, and Religion at the University of Gothenburg, Sweden, has contributed with both time, space, and resources for the final language editing. When it is published, however, I will have moved to the Faculty of Theology at the University of Oslo, Norway. I wish to acknowledge the support I have received from these two institutions to produce this book, but most of all the atmosphere of collegiality that distinguishes them both.

Ola Sigurdson, April 2024

Abramovic, Marina (2016). *Walk Through Walls: A Memoir*. London: Fig Tree.

Adorno, Theodor W. (1997). *Aesthetic Theory*. Translated by Robert Hullot-Kentor. London/New York: Continuum.

Albertsen, Niels (1999). "Urbane atmosfærer". In *Sosiologi i dag*, nr 4, pp. 5–29.

Amin, Ash, and Thrift, Nigel (2002). *Cities: Reimagining the Urban*. Cambridge/Malden: Polity Press.

– (2016). *Seeing Like a City*. Cambridge/Malden: Polity Press.

Assmann, Jan (2007). *Das kulturelle Gedächtnis: Schrift, Erinnerung und politische Identität in frühen Hochkulturen*. Sixth edition. München: Verlag C.H. Beck.

Augé, Marc (1995). *Non-Places: Introduction to an Anthropology of Supermodernity*. Translated by John Howe. London/New York: Verso.

Bachelard, Gaston (1988). *Air and Dreams: An Essay on the Imagination of Movement*. Translated by Edith Farrell and Frederick Farrell. Dallas: Dallas Institute Publications.

– (1994). *The Poetics of Space*. Translated by Maria Jolas. Boston: Beacon Press.

– (2020). *La poetique de l'espace*. Ed. Gilles Hieronimus. Paris: Presses Universitaires de France.

Bakerson, Aram (2010). *Från järnvägsstation till kommunikationsnod: En studie av verksamhetsfunktioner, rumsliga komponenter och anpassning till nutida resandebehov i järnvägsstationer från sju länder*. Göteborg: Chalmers tekniska högskola, diss.

Baumgarten, Alexander G. (2007). *Ästhetik*. Band 1. Ed. Dagmar Mirbach. Hamburg: Felix Meiner Verlag.

Benjamin, Walter (1977). "Das Kunstwerk im Zeitalter seiner technischen Reproduzierbarkeit". In *Illuminationen: Ausgewählte Schriften 1*. Frankfurt am Main: Suhrkamp, pp. 136–169.

– (1991). *The Arcades Project*. Translated by Howard Eiland and Kevin McLaughlin. Cambridge/London: The Belknap Press.

Blumenberg, Hans (2018). *Theorie der Unbegrifflichkeit*. Third edition. Frankfurt am Main: Suhrkamp.

Bollnow, Otto Friedrich (2001). *Die pädagogische Atmosphäre*. Essen: Die Blaue Eule.

– (2009). *Das Wesen der Stimmungen. Schriften Band 1*. Würzburg: Königshausen & Neumann.

– (2010). *Mensch und Raum*. Eleventh edition. Stuttgart: Kohlhammer.

– (2011). *Human Space*. Translated by Christine Shuttleworth. London: Hyphen Press.

Borch, Christian (ed. 2014). *Architectural Atmospheres: On the Experience and Politics of Architecture*. Basel: Birkhäuser.

Bornemark, Jonna, and Svenaeus, Fredrik (ed. 2009). *Vad är praktisk kunskap?* Södertörn Studies in Practical Knowledge 1. Huddinge: Södertörns högskola.

Böhme, Gernot (1989). *Für eine ökologische Naturästhetik*. Frankfurt am Main: Suhrkamp.

– (1998). *Anmutungen: Über das Atmosphärische*. Stuttgart: Edition Tertium.

– (2001). *Aisthetik: Vorlesungen über Ästhetik als allgemeine Wahrnehmungslehre*. München: Fink.

– (2008). ”Phänomenologie als Kritik”. In *Neue Phänomenologie zwischen Praxis und Theorie: Festschrift für Hermann Schmitz*. Ed. Michael Großheim. Freiburg/München: Verlag Karl Alber, pp. 21–36.

– (2013). *Architektur und Atmosphäre*. Second edition. München: Fink.

– (2016). *Ästhetischer Kapitalismus*. Frankfurt am Main: Suhrkamp.

– (2019a). *Atmosphäre: Essays zur neuen Ästhetik*. Fourth edition. Frankfurt am Main: Suhrkamp.

– (2019b). *Der Leib: Die Natur, die wir selbst sind*. Frankfurt am Main: Suhrkamp.

Brindle, Steven (2004). *Paddington Station: Its History and Architecture*. Swindon: English Heritage.

– (2008). “I. K. Brunel – First Among Equals?”. In *Transactions of the Newcomen Society*, 78:1, pp. 11–23.

Canepa, Elisabetta (2022). *Architecture Is Atmosphere*. Milano: Mimesis International.

Casey, Edward S. (1997). *The Fate of Place: A Philosophical History*. Berkeley/Los Angeles/London: University of California Press.

Certeau, Michel de (1990). *L'invention du quotidien: 1. Arts de faire*. New edition. Paris: Gallimard.

Certeau, Michel de (1984). *The Practice of Everyday Life*. Translation by Steven Rendall. Berkeley/Los Angeles/London: University of California Press.

Chrétien, Jean-Louis (2003). *Hand to Hand: Listening to the Work of Art*. Translated by Stephen E. Lewis. New York: Fordham University Press.

Christiansen, Rupert (2018). *City of Light: The Making of Modern Paris*. New York: Basic Books.

Coccia, Emanuele (2021). *Filosofia della casa: Lo spazio domestico e la felicità*. Turin: Einaudi.

Connerton, Paul (1989). *How Societies Remember*. Cambridge: Cambridge University Press.

Cornell, Peter (1997). *Saker: Om tingens synlighet*. New Edition. Hedemora: Gidlunds.

Costa, C., Carmenates, S., Madeira, L., and Stanghellini, G. (2014). "Phenomenology of atmospheres: The felt meanings of clinical encounters". In *Journal of Psychopathology*, 20:4, pp. 351–357.

Courbin, Alain (1982). *Le miasme et la jonquille: L'odorat et l'imaginaire social. 18e–19e siècles*. Paris: Aubier-Montaigne.

Crary, Jonathan (2013). *24/7: Late Capitalism and the Ends of Sleep*. London: Verso.

Dahl, Espen (2010). *Phenoomenology and the Holy: Religious Experience after Husserl*. London: SCM.

Dahlberg, Göran (2009). *Att umgås med spöken*. Stockholm: Ruin.

Dahlberg, Göran (2010). *Hemliga städer: Rädslans urbana former*. Glänta Hardcore 04. Göteborg: Glänta produktion.

Davies, Owen (2007). *The Haunted: A Social History of Ghosts*. New York: Palgrave Macmillan.

DeLaine, Janet (1999). "The *Romanitas of* the Railway Station". In *Uses and Abuses of Antiquity*. Ed. Michael D. Biddniss and Maria Wyke. Bern: Peter Lang.

Desmond, William (1995). *Being and the Between*. Albany: State University of New York Press.

Dreyfus, Hubert L. (2008). *On the Internet*. Second edition. London/New York: Routledge.

Eliade, Mircea (1959). *The Sacred and the Profane: The Nature of Religion*. Translated by Willard R. Trask. Orlando: Harcourt, Brace Company.

Fischer-Lichte, Erika (2008). *The Transformative Power of Performance: A New Aesthetics*. Translated by Saskya Iris Jain. London/New York: Routledge.

– (2012). "Transforming Spectators into *Viri Perculsi*: Baroque Theatre as Machinery for Producing Affects". In *Performativity and Performance in Baroque Rome*. Ed. Peter Gillgren and Mårten Snickare. Farnham/Burlington: Ashgate, pp. 87–97.

Fischer-Lichte, Erika (2019). *Ästhetik des Performativen*. Eleventh edition. Frankfurt am Main: Suhrkamp.

Forsell, Håkan (2020). *Den föränderliga staden*. RJ:s årsbox 2020. Göteborg/Stockholm: Makadam förlag.

Foucault, Michel (1986). "Of Other Spaces". In *Diacritics*, 16:1, pp. 22–27.

Freedberg, David, and Gallese, Vittorio (2007). "Motion, emotion and empathy in esthetic experience". In *Trends in Cognitive Science*, 11:5, pp. 197–203.

Freud, Sigmund (1955). "The Uncanny". In *An Infantile Neurosis and Other Works*. Translation by James Strachey. London: Hogarth Press, pp. 218–252.

Fuchs, Thomas (2018). *Leib, Raum, Person: Entwurf einer phänomenologischen Anthropologie*. Second edition. Stuttgart: Klett-Cotta.

Funke, Dieter (2014). *Die dritte Haut: Psychoanalyse des Wohnens*. Second edition. Gießen: Psychosozial-Verlag.

Gallese, Vittorio (2015). "Architectural Space from Within: The Body, Space and the Brain". In *Architecture and Empathy*. Ed. Philip Tidwell. Esbo: Tapio Wirkkala Rut Bryk Foundation, pp. 64–77.

Gammelgaard Nielsen, Anders (2021). *Atmosfære og byggekultur – Atmosphere and Building Culture*. Köpenhamn: Arkitekturforlaget B.

Giedion, Sigfried (1967). *Space, Time and Architecture: The Growth of a New Tradition*. Fifth editon. Cambridge: Harvard University Press.

Glück, Louise (2014). "Cornwall". In *Faithful and Virtuous Night*. New York: Farrar, Straus and Giroux.

Goethe, Johann Wolfgang (1970). *Aus meinem Leben: Dichtung und Wahrheit. Band 1: Text*. Ed. Siegfried Scheibe. Berlin: Akademie-Verlag.

– (2013). *Italienische Reise*. Third edition. Frankfurt am Main: Fischer Taschenbuch Verlag.

Gombrich, Ernest H. (2006). *The Story of Art*. Paperback. London: Phaidon.

Griffero, Tonino (2010). *Atmosferologia: Estetica degli Spazi Emozionali*. Milano/Udine: Mimesis Edizioni.

– (2013). *Quasi-cose: La realtà dei sentimenti*. Milano: Bruno Mondadori.

– (2014). "Architectural Affordances: The Atmospheric Authority of Spaces". In *Architecture and Atmosphere*. Ed. Philip Tidwell. Esbo: Tapio Wirkkala Rut Bryk Foundation, pp. 15–47.

– (2019). "Introduction: How Do You Find Yourself In Your Environment? Hermann Schmitz's New Phenomenology". In Hermann Schmitz. *New Phenomenology: A Brief Introduction*. Milano: Mimesis International, pp. 9–41.

– (2020). *Places, Affordances, Atmospheres: A Pathic Aesthetics*. London/New York: Routledge.

– (2021). *The Atmospherical "We": Moods and Collective Feelings*. Milano: Mimesis International.

Grote, Simon (2017). *The Emergence of Modern Aesthetic Theory: Religion and Morality in Enlightenment Germany and Scotland*. Cambridge: Cambridge University Press.

Gumbrecht, Hans Ulrich (2004). *Production of Presence: What Meaning Cannot Convey*. Stanford: Stanford University Press.

– (2011). *Stimmungen lesen: Über eine verdeckte Wirklichkeit der Literatur*. München: Carl Hanser Verlag.

– (2012). *Atmosphere, Mood, Stimmung: On a Hidden Potential of Literature*. Stanford: Standford University Press.

– (2020). *Crowds: Das Stadion als Ritual von Intensität*. Klostermann Essay 5. Frankfurt am Main: Vittorio Klostermann.

Guzzoni, Ute (2017). *Wohnen und Wandern*. München: Verlag Karl Alber.

Han, Byung-Chul (2021). *Infokratie: Digitalisierung und die Krise der Demokratie*. Second edition. Berlin: Matthes & Seitz.

Harrison, Robert Pogue (1992). *Forests: The Shadow of Civilization*. Chicago/London: University of Chicago Press.

– (2008). *Gardens: An Essay on the Human Condition*. Chicago/London: University of Chicago Press.

Hartmann, Martin (2010). *Gefühle: Wie die Wissenschaften sie erklären*. Second edition. Frankfurt/New York: Campus Verlag.

Hasse, Jürgen (2015a). *Der Leib der Stadt: Phänomenographische Annäherungen*. Freiburg/München: Verlag Karl Alber.

– (2015b). *Was Räume mit uns machen – und wir mit ihnen: Kritische Phänomenologie des Raumes*. Second edition. München: Verlag Karl Alber.

– (2020). *Wohnungswechsel: Phänomenologie des Ein- und Auswohnens.* Bielefeld: Transcript Verlag.

Hegel, G. W. F. (1990). *Vorlesungen über die Ästhetik II. Werke 14.* Frankfurt am Main: Suhrkamp.

Heidegger, Martin (1977). *Sein und Zeit. Gesamtausgabe. 1 Abteilung. Band 2.* Frankfurt am Main: Vittorio Klostermann.

– (2000). "Bauen Wohnen Denken". In *Vorträge und Aufsätze (1936–1953). Gestamtausgabe. Band 7.* Ed. Friedrich-Wilhelm von Herrmann. Frankfurt am Main: Vittorio Klostermann, pp. 145–164.

Huizing, Klaas (2022). *Lebenslehre. Eine Theologie für das 21. Jahrhundert.* Gütersloh: Gütersloher Verlagshaus.

Husserl, Edmund (1996). *Die Krisis der europäischen Wissenschaften und die transzendentale Phänomenologie: Eine Einleitung in die phänomenologische Philosophie.* Ed. Elisabeth Ströker. Third edition. Hamburg: Felix Meiner Verlag.

Ingold, Tim (2015). *The Life of Lines.* London/New York: Routledge.

Jay, Martin (1993). *Downcast Eyes: The Denigration of Vision in Twentieth-Century French Thought.* Berkeley/Los Angeles/London: University of California Press.

Jenkyns, Richard (2013). *God, Space, and City in the Roman Imagination.* Oxford: Oxford University Press.

Joas, Hans (2017). *Die Macht des Heiligen: Eine Alternative zur Geschichte von der Entzauberung.* Frankfurt am Main: Suhrkamp.

Kant, Immanuel (2000). *Critique of the Power of Judgement.* Translated by Paul Guyer and Eric Matthews. Cambridge: Cambridge University Press.

Karlsson, Ingmar, and Ruth, Arne (1983). *Samhället som teater: Estetik och politik i Tredje riket.* Stockholm: Liber förlag.

Kieckhefer, Richard (2004). *Theology in Stone: Church Architecture from Byzantium to Berkeley.* Oxford: Oxford University Press.

Kierkegaard, Søren (1991). *Afsluttende uvidenskabelig Efterskrift til de philosophiske Smuler. Første halvbind. Samlade værker. Band 9.* Ed. A. B. Drachmann, J. L. Heiberg and H. O. Lange. Köpenhamn: Gyldendal.

Kilde, Jeanne Halgren (2008). *Sacred Power, Sacred Space: An Introduction to Christian Architecture and Worship.* Oxford: Oxford University Press.

Kittler, Friedrich (1995). *Aufschreibesysteme 1800, 1900.* Third edition. München: Fink.

Lagerkvist Amanda (2022). *Existential Media: A Media Theory of the Limit Situation.* New York: Oxford University Press.

Landzelius, Michael (2009). "Spatial reification, or, collectively embodied amnesia, aphasia, and apraxia". In *Semiotica,* 175:1, pp. 39–75.

Lauter, Jörg (2014). *Die Verzauberung der Welt: Eine Kulturgeschichte des Christentums.* Munich: Verlag C. H. Beck.

Le Corbusier (1923). *Vers une architecture.* Second edition. Paris: Les Éditions G. Cres et Cie.

Le Corbusier (1986). *Towards a New Architecture.* Translated by Frederick Etchells. Garden City: Dover Publications.

Leeuw, Gerardus van der (1986). *Religion in Essence and Manifestation*. Translated by J. E. Turner: Princeton: Princeton University Press.

Lefebvre, Henri (1991). *The Production of Space*. Translated by Donald Nicholson-Smith. Malden/Oxford: Blackwells.

Lindemann, Gesa, and Schünemann, David (2020). "Presence in Digital Spaces: A Phenomenological Concept of Presence in Mediatized Communication". In *Human Studies*, 43:4, pp. 627–651.

Luckhurst, Roger (2019). *Corridors: Passages of Modernity*. London: Reaktion Books.

McCarraher, Eugene (2019). *The Enchantments of Mammon: How Capitalism Became the Religion of Modernity*. Cambridge/London: The Belknapp Press.

MacDonald, William L. (1976). *The Pantheon: Design, Meaning and Progeny*. Cambridge: Harvard University Press.

Madsen, Theis Vallø (2019). "De-scripting a Museum's Presence and Atmosphere: An exhibition Experiment". In *Museum & Society*, 17:2, pp. 229–247.

Maier, Andreas (2015). *Die Straße: Roman*. Frankfurt am Main: Suhrkamp.

Maier, Jessica (2020). *The Eternal City: A History of Rome in Maps*. Chicago: University of Chicago Press.

Mallgrave, Harry Francis (2022). *Building Paradise: Episodes in Paradisiacal Thinking*. New York/London: Routledge.

Marder, Tod A., and Wilson Jones, Mark (ed. 2015). *The Pantheon: From Antiquity to the Present*. New York/Cambridge: Cambridge University Press.

Merleau-Ponty, Maurice (1945). *Phénoménologie de la perception*. Paris: Gallimard.

– (1964). "Cézanne's Doubt". In *Sense and Non-Sense*. Translated by Hubert L. Dreyfus and Patricia Allen Dreyfus. Evanston: Northwestern University Press, pp. 9–25.

– (1992). *Phenomenology of Perception*. Translated by Colin Smith. London: Routledge.

Mumford, Lewis (1989). *The City in History: Its Origins, Its Transformations, and Its Prospects*. San Diego/New York/London: A Harvest Book.

Nietzsche, Friedrich (1996). *Human, All too Human*. Translated by R. J. Hollingdale. Cambridge: Cambridge University Press.

Norberg-Schulz, Christian (1980). *Genius Loci: Towards a Phenomenology of Architecture*. New York: Rizzoli.

Nordholm, Johannes (2017). "Alltets rum: Hadrianus arkitektur i Rom". In *Arche: Tidskrift för psykoanalys, humaniora och arkitektur*, nr 60–61.

Nordström, Ludvig (1928). *Lort-Sverige*. Third edition. Stockholm: Kooperativa förbundets bokförlag.

Otero-Pailos, Jorge (2007). "Photo[historio]graphy: Christian Norberg-Schultz's Demotion of Textual History". In *Journal of the Society of Architectural Historians*, 66:2, pp. 220–241.

Otto, Rudolf (1958). *The Idea of the Holy*. Translated by John W. Harvey. London/Oxford/New York: Oxford University Press.

Otto, Rudolf (2014). *Das Heilige: Über das Irrationale in der Idee des Göttlichen und sein Verhältnis zum Rationalen*. New edition. München: C. H. Beck.

Pallasmaa, Juhani (2009). *The Thinking Hand: Existential and Embodied Wisdom in Architecture*. Chichester: Wiley.

– (2011). *The Embodied Image: Imagination and Imagery in Architecture*. Chichester: Wiley.

– (2012). *The Eyes of the Skin: Architecture and the Senses*. Third edition. Chichester: Wiley.

Perec, Georges (2008). *Species of Spaces and Other Pieces*. Translated by John Sturrock. London: Penguin.

Perullo, Nicola (2021). *Epistenologia: Il vino come filosofia*. Milano: Mimesis.

Plessner, Helmut (1975). *Die Stufen des Organischen und der Mensch: Einführung in die philosophische Anthropologie*. Third edition. Berlin/New York, NY: Walter de Gruyter.

Rauh, Andreas (2012). *Die besondere Atmosphäre: Ästhetische Feldforschungen*. Bielefeld: Transcript Verlag.

Renhardt, Volker (2014). *Geschichte Roms: Von der Antike bis zur Gegenwart*. Second edition. Munich: C. H. Beck.

Ricœur, Paul (1995). "Manifestation and Proclamation". In *Figuring the Sacred: Religion, Narrative, and Imagination*. Ed. Mark I. Wallace. Minneapolis: Fortress.

Riedel, Friedlind (2019). "Atmosphere". In *Affective Societies: Key Concepts*. Ed. Jan Slaby and Christian von Scheve. London/New York: Routledge, pp. 85–95.

Robinson, Sarah (2015). "Boundaries of the Skin: John Dewey, Didier Anzieu and Architectural Possibility". In *Architecture and Empathy*. Ed. Philip Tidwell. Esbo: Tapio Wirkkala Rut Bryk Foundation, pp. 43–63.

Rosa, Hartmut (2017). "Resonanzen im Zeitalter der Digitalisierung". In *Medien Journal*, 41:1, pp. 15–25.

– (2020). *Resonanz: Eine Soziologie der Weltbeziehung*. Third edition. Frankfurt am Main: Suhrkamp.

– (2020b). *Unverfügbarkeit*. Seventh Edition. Vienna/Salzburg: Residenz Verlag.

Ruskin, John (2009). *Selected Writings*. Ed. Dinah Birch. Oxford World's Classics. Oxford: Oxford University Press.

Rykwert, Joseph (2009). *The Seduction of Place: The History and Future of the City*. New York: Oxford University Press.

– (2010). *The Idea of a Town: The Anthropology of Urban Form in Rome, Italy and the Ancient World*. London: Faber and Faber.

Sacasas, L. M. (2020). "The Analog City and the Digital City: How online life breaks the old political order". In *The New Atlantis*, nr 61, pp. 3–18.

Samuel, Flora, and Linder-Gaillard, Inge (2020). *Sacred Concrete: The Churches of Le Corbusier*. Second revised edition. Basel: Birkhäuser.

Sand, Monica (2019). *Tro, hopp och konst – konst som politiskt verktyg: Forskningsrapport om Statens konstråds satsning Konst händer 2016–2018*. Stockholm: ArkDes.

Saint-Exupéry, Antoine de (2000). *Southern Mail/Night Flight*. Translated by Curtis Cate. Penguin Classics. London: Penguin Books.

Schiller, Friedrich (2002). *Über die ästhetische Erziehung des Menschen in einer Reihe von Briefen*. Stuttgart: Reclam.

Schmitz, Hermann (1999). *Adolf Hitler in der Geschichte*. Bonn: Bouvier.

– (2003). *Was ist Neue Phänomenologie?*. Rostock: Ingo Koch Verlag.

– (2016). *Atmosphären*. Second edition. Freiburg/München: Verlag Karl Alber.

– (2019a). *Das Göttliche und der Raum. System der Philosophie, bd III/4*. München: Verlag Karl Alber.

– (2019b). *Der Gefühlsraum. System der Philosophie, bd III/2*. München: Verlag Karl Alber.

– (2019c). *Der Leib. System der Philosophie, bd II/1*. München: Verlag Karl Alber.

– (2019d). *Die Wahrnehmung. System der Philosophie, bd III/5*. München: Verlag Karl Alber.

– (2019e) *New Phenomenology: A Brief Introduction*. Milano: Mimesis International.

– (2019f). *System der Philosophie*. Five volumes in ten parts. New edition. München: Verlag Karl Alber.

Schwartz, Rudolf (1947). *Vom Bau der Kirche*. Second edition. Heidelberg: Verlag Lambert Schneider.

Sedlmayr, Hans (2001). *Die Entstehung der Kathedrale*. Wiesbaden: VMA-Verlag.

Sennett, Richard (2009). *The Craftsman*. London: Penguin Books.

Sharr, Adam (2018). *Modern Architecture: A Very Short Introduction*. Oxford: Oxford University Press.

Sigurdson, Ola (2001). *De prudentia: Om principer och personer i etiken*. Stockholm/Stehag: Brutus Östlings bokförlag Symposion.

– (2012). *Theology and Marxism in Eagleton and Žižek: A Conspiracy of Hope*. New York: Palgrave Macmillan.

– (2016). *Heavenly Bodies: Incarnation, the Gaze, and Embodiment in Christian Theology*. Translated by Carl Olsen. Grand Rapids: Eerdmans.

– (2020). ”I händelsernas mitt: Om relationen mellan filosofi och teologi”. In *Arche: Tidskrift för psykoanalys, humaniora, konst och arkitektur*, nr 70–71, pp. 144–151.

– (2021). ”Vardagslivets psykoteologi: Om subjektivitet och transcendens”. In *Arche: Tidskrift för psykoanalys, humaniora, konst och arkitektur*, nr 76–77, pp. 171–182.

– (2021b). *Gudomliga komedier: Humor, subjektivitet, transcendens: Volym 3: Kritik av den existentiella humorn*. Göteborg: Glänta.

– (2022). "Arkitektur som tredje hud: Om rum, kropp och atmosfär". In *Rhetorica Scandinavica*, nr 84, pp. 94–110.

– (2024). *Trösklar: En kritisk genomgång*. Stockholm/Umeå: Andersson Örn.

Simmel, Georg (2001). "Brücke und Tür". In *Aufsätze und Abhandlingen 1909–1918. Band 1. Gestamtausgabe Band 12*. Frankfurt am Main: Suhrkamp, pp. 55–61.

– (2002). "The Metropolis and Mental Life". In *The Blackwell City Reader*. Ed. Gary Bridge and Sophie Watson. Malden: Blackwell, pp. 11–19.

– (2020). *Die Großstädte und das Geistesleben*. Second Edition. Frankfurt am Main: Suhrkamp.

Smith, Jonathan Z. (1987). *To Take Place: Toward a Theory in Ritual.* Chicago/London: University of Chicago Press.

Snickare, Mårten (2012). "How to Do Things with the Piazza San Pietro: Performativity and Baroque Architecture". In *Performativity and Performance in Baroque Rome.* Ed. Peter Gillgren and Mårten Snickare. Farnham/Burlington: Ashgate, pp. 65–83.

Solnit, Rebecca (2005). *A Field Guide to Getting Lost.* New York: Viking.

Spitzer, Leo (1942). "Milieu and Ambiance: An Essay in Historical Semantics". In *Philosophy and Phenomenological Research,* 3:2, pp. 169–218.

– (1963). *Classical and Christian Ideas of World Harmony: Prolegomena to an Interpretation of the Word "Stimmung".* Baltimore: Johns Hopkins University Press.

Ströker, Elisabeth (1977). *Philosophische Untersuchungen zum Raum.* Second edition. Frankfurt am Main: Klostermann.

Thibaud, Jean-Paul (2015a). *En quête d'ambiances: Éprouver la ville en passant.* Genève: MētisPresses.

– (2015b). "The Sensory Fabric of Urban Ambiances". In *The Senses and Society,* 6:2, pp. 203–215.

Tidwell, Philip (ed. 2014). *Architecture and Atmosphere.* Esbo: Tapio Wirkkala Rut Bryk Foundation.

Trenter, Stieg (1945). *I dag röd …* Stockholm: Albert Bonniers Förlag.

Tschudi, Victor Plahte (2015). "Goethe in the Hall and His Journeys in Printed Room". In *Architectural Histories,* 3:1, pp. 1–17.

Tuan, Yi-Fu (1977). *Space and Place: The Perspective of Experience.* Minneapolis/London: University of Minnesota Press.

"Ville sauvage" (2022). *Billebaude,* nr 20.

Vitruvius (1955). *On Architecture: Books I–V.* Translated by Frank Granger. Loeb Classical Library. Harvard University Press.

Waldenfels, Bernhard (2012). *Hyperphänomene: Modi hyperbolischer Erfahrung.* Frankfurt am Main: Suhrkamp.

Wellbery, David E. (2010). "Stimmung". In Ästhetische *Grundbegriffe. Band 5: Postmoderne bis Synästhesie.* Ed. Karlheinz Barck, Martin Fontius, Dieter Schlenstedt, Burkhart Steinwachs and Friedrich Wolfzettel. Stuttgard/Weimar: J. B. Metzler, pp. 703–733.

Wolf, Jakob (2017). *Krob og atmosfærer: Hermann Schmitz'nye fænomenologi.* Köpenhamn: Eksistensen.

Woolf, Virginia (2000). *A Room of One's Own.* London: Penguin.

Zumthor, Peter (2006). *Atmosphären: Architektonische Umgebungen: Die Dinge um mich herum.* Basel: Birkhäuser.

– (2017). *Architektur Denken.* Third expanded edition. Basel: Birkhäuser.

*Digital Sources*

"Atmospheric Spaces". https://atmosphericspaces.wordpress.com. Access 240109.
"Gesellschaft für Neue Phänomenologie". https://www.gnp-online.de/die-gnp/die-gesellschaft.html. Access 240109.
Palumbo, Jacqui (2020). "The Pantheon: The ancient building still being used after 2000 years". *CNN*, 16 November. https://edition.cnn.com/style/article/pantheon-history-test-of- time/index.html. Access 240109.
"Researching Atmospheres". https://pure.au.dk/portal/files/53695533/RESEARCHING_ATMOSPHERES.pdf. Access 240109.

Printed by
Rotomail Italia S.P.A.
June 2024